AF076376

THE GOTHAM GRAMMARIAN

Gary Lutz

Ⓢ 2015 Gary Lutz. Copyleft—all rites reversed.

ISBN: 978-1-940853-07-9

This book may be freely reproduced, adapted, repurposed, etc., as long as it is under these same copyleft conditions (not to be copyrighted or reproduced for profit or commercial gain).

Cover and art by Mark McCormick.

Published by Calamari Archive, Inc.

NY, NY

www.calamariarchive.com

Contents

Introduction 4

Verbal Agreements 5

Placement Services 18

Pronouns Are Not for Amateurs 29

Countererrorist Measures 42

The Comma-ist Manifesto 69

Punctuational Punctilio 92

A Miscellany of Malpractice 112

Introduction

The most brilliant writers occasionally stumble with grammar and punctuation, and the rest of us can learn from their missteps.

The Gotham Grammarian is a book of rules and guidelines for anyone who believes that correctness and precision still matter. The book discusses the ninety-five errors that most often go undetected by stellar writers, as well as by editors, copy editors, and proofreaders.

The erroneous examples (which are preceded by a banana-peel icon) have been drawn from distinguished newspapers and magazines, as well as from books brought out by distinguished publishing houses. I am sure to have committed my own share of blunders in writing this book.

An index to *The Gotham Grammarian*, as well as a glossary of grammatical terms, will appear online at http://www.gothamgrammarian.com, and an unabridged version of the book may eventually be available electronically.

Anyone interested in reading further about syntax, grammar, punctuation, and usage is urged to become a lifelong companion of *Garner's Modern American Usage*, by Bryan A. Garner (third edition, Oxford University Press, 2009); *Modern American Usage: A Guide*, by Wilson Follett (Hill and Wang, 1966); *The Careful Writer*, by Theodore M. Bernstein (Free Press, 1995); *The Handbook of Good English*, by Edward D. Johnson (Washington Square Press, 1991); and *Understanding Grammar*, by Paul Roberts (Harper & Row, 1954).

Finally, I express my deepest gratitude to the publisher, Derek White, and to Jane Unrue for their acute editorial attentions. I also thank Gordon Lish, E. M., Thomas Vasko, and Lisel Virkler.

Verbal Agreements

1 Don't let the object of a preposition become the object of your affection.

A lone noun serving as the subject of a clause is often followed by at least one prepositional phrase, whose purpose is to add details or texture to the statement. Each of those prepositional phrases trailing behind the subject will have at least one noun or pronoun functioning as the object of the preposition. Unfortunately, a writer can easily mistake any of those objects for the subject, especially when an object is the noun or pronoun appearing immediately before the verb.

The verb of a clause must agree in number with the subject, not with an object. With rare exceptions (discussed in Chapters 14 and 15), the object of a preposition does not determine the singularity or plurality of the verb; the singularity or plurality of the subject alone makes that determination. So it's best to develop the habit of not giving prepositional phrases the time of day. If you keep your eye on the subject, you're sure to choose the appropriate form of the verb.

Below are sentences in which writers lost track of the subjects and were thrown off by objects of prepositions trying to hog the spotlight. As a result, the writers committed errors in subject-verb agreement. In each example, the subject of the troublesome clause is boldfaced, the one or more distracting prepositional phrases are underlined, and the erroneous verb is italicized. The plural verb in each excerpt must be singularized.

 … the **success** <u>of sites such as Netflix and Spotify</u> *show* that, at least with some goods, renting can trump ownership. (*New Yorker*)

 Stark's new **show** <u>of sculpturally collaged works on paper</u>, mostly white but splashed with plumage-like color, *explore* a vanishing pink-collar world. (*New Yorker*)

 Even if Faulkner isn't your thing, or if **confusion** <u>of characters and time frames</u> *aren't*, either, it's important to see the piece…. (*New Yorker*)

2 My mother, in addition to her mother, as well as my dearest aunt, along with her son, plus my only surviving uncle, *is*—not *are*—invited to learn this rule.

In Chapter 1, you learned to ignore objects of prepositions when you're deciding whether the verb of a clause should be singular or plural. Most prepositions are single words, but our language also includes a few multiword prepositions, often called complex prepositions, which can cause writers much conjugational distress. The most common are *in addition to, along with,* and *as well as*. You must treat them like all other prepositions. The same is true of the prepositional use of *plus* (a word best avoided except in arithmetical contexts) and *combined with* and *coupled with*. Turn your back on the objects of multiword prepositions (and of any prepositional equivalents) when you're conjugating verbs. The italicized verbs in the following excerpts are incorrect and must be singularized. Subjects are boldfaced; prepositional phrases are underlined.

 **Gospel**, <u>along with New Orleans jazz and R. & B.</u>, *influence* the work of the pianist and vocalist Butler in profound ways.... (*New Yorker*)

 This **arrangement**, <u>plus a duplicate of Lennon's lead vocal</u>, *were* added on takes 9 and 10. (*Revolution in the Head: The Beatles' Records and the Sixties* [Henry Holt], by Ian MacDonald)

 Widespread **access** to unhealthy foods, <u>coupled with sedentary behavior brought on by wealth and the absence of a dieting and exercise culture</u>, *have* caused obesity levels ... to approach or even exceed those in Western countries. (*Wall Street Journal*)

3 Don't let complements go to your head.

We often write sentences whose message boils down to $A = B$, such as *Kelsey is an endodontist*. The subject (*Kelsey*) is being equated with another noun (*endodontist*) by a verb commonly known as a linking verb (*is*), though it's also classified as an equational verb, because it functions like an equal sign. The noun equated with the subject by the equational verb is called a complement. (A complement is something that completes something else; we say, for instance, that a particular wine is the perfect complement to an entrée.)

A complement is a highly visible noun that often monopolizes a writer's attention when the time comes to conjugate the verb of a clause. The writer too easily succumbs to making the verb agree with the complement instead of with the subject. That sort of blunder is most likely to occur when the subject of a clause is singular and the complement is plural.

 ...the only **ornamentation**, aside from flashes of embroidery on the mostly dark clothes, *were* jeweled <u>buttons</u>. (*New York Times*)

The subject is the singular noun *ornamentation*; the complement is the plural noun *buttons*. The verb must therefore be *was*.

The rule is simple: don't fall for a complement. Keep your head—and don't let the subject out of your sight. The singularity or plurality of the subject determines whether the verb should be singular or plural. The complement has no influence at all.

In the following sentences, the subjects of independent clauses are boldfaced, the misconjugated verbs are italicized, and the complements are underlined. Each italicized verb must be singularized.

 One **thing** she didn't involve herself in *were* the theater's financial <u>affairs</u>. (*Pauline Kael: A Life in the Dark* [Viking], by Brian Kellow)

 His most distinctive **contribution** *were* the <u>hundreds</u> of small drawings he produced weekly.... (*The Art of* The New Yorker, *1925-1995* [Knopf], by Lee Lorenz)

4 Disagreeable Appositives

Appositives, if not treated with care, can wreak all manner of grammatical and punctuational havoc on a sentence, and a variety of such disturbances will be discussed throughout this book. Right now, though, it will suffice if we understand an appositive as nothing more than a noun, or a phrase functioning as a noun, that typically follows another noun and offers the reader a little bouquet of information about that noun. In the sentence *She moved to Cobble Hill, her favorite neighborhood,* the appositive is *her favorite neighborhood.*

The subject of a clause—and not the appositive following it—determines whether the verb should be singular or plural. But a plural appositive following a singular subject sometimes leads a writer to pluralize the verb. In each of the following excerpts, the subject is boldfaced, the appositive is underlined, and the erroneous verb, in italics, must be singularized.

 The changing **nature** of technology—<u>cloud-based applications in particular</u>—*enable* new start-ups to succeed more quickly.... (*Wall Street Journal*)

 [William] Burroughs's **work,** <u>especially his experimental cut-up novels,</u> *are* an important influence on many of the musicians involved.... (*New Yorker*) [Here, though, the writer could easily pluralize the subject and retain the plural verb.]

5 Putting One and One Together

The subject of a clause often consists of two or more nouns (or noun phrases or, occasionally, even nominative dependent clauses) joined by the coordinating conjunction *and.* Think of *and* as a plus sign. Subjects taking the form *A and B,* therefore, almost always require a plural verb—in much the same way that 1 + 1 = 2, not 1. Let's call such subjects additive-compound subjects. In additive-compound subjects, *A* and *B* typically name two appreciably different things, characteristics, or qualities, and thus a singular verb would strike attentive readers as dead wrong. In the following excerpts, the nouns constituting the additive-compound subjects are underlined, and the erroneous verbs, in italics, must be reconjugated.

 The <u>number</u> and <u>size</u> of New York's drag balls in the 1920s and 1930s *indicates* the cohesion and scale of the gay world in those years. (*Gay New York: Gender, Urban Culture, and the Making of the Gay Male World, 1890-1940* [Basic Books], by George Chauncey)

 To be sure, we've always had sports heroes...whose sly <u>irony</u> and authority-defining <u>insouciance</u> *lends* them the adolescent glamour of Peck's Bad Boy.... (*The Atlantic*)

–7–

 Knight assembled a crew of Tea Partiers, Ayn Rand obsessives, and the like into an improvised dance troupe, in which Sarah Palin <u>ventriloquism</u> and twitchy <u>choreography</u> *intermingles* with the participants' stunningly selfish assertions. (*New Yorker*)

The same principle applies to an additive-compound subject consisting of three or more elements.

 A green-and-purple neon <u>sign</u>, a neon-caked <u>bar</u> offering a bajillion tequilas, and a gaudy <u>triptych</u> of, one supposes, the goddess of toloache, *beckons* spendthrift tourists.... (*New Yorker*) [The final comma must be deleted.]

That an additive-compound subject requires a plural verb would seem to be one of the simplest rules of them all. But the number of exceptions to the rule can be daunting. Following are six guidelines to help you choose between plural and singular verbs. (A proviso, though: if your verb choice bothers you even a little, you can expect that it will bother at least some readers a lot.)

First, if *A* and *B* are nearly equivalent in meaning or if *B* renames *A*, a singular verb is unchallengeable.

 The company's unexpected <u>comeback</u> and its <u>rebound</u> in profits is good news to shareholders.

Second, if *A* and *B* blend into each other to such a degree that they form a single entity in your thinking (as in familiar expressions such as *living and learning* and *forgiving and forgetting*), choose a singular verb.

 <u>Trial</u> and <u>error</u> *play* an inevitable role. (*New York Times*)

Third, if *A* and *B* are nouns expressing opposites and, taken together, form a whole (as in *the long and short of it*), or if the two nouns express the dual nature of a single thing (as in *its blessing and its curse*), a singular verb is correct.

Fourth, an additive-compound subject expressing two closely related phases or stages of a single process (such as *waxing and waning* or *texting and driving*) requires a singular verb.

 One group was then told that <u>failure</u> and <u>trying again</u> *are* part of the learning process. (*Wall Street Journal*)

An additive-compound subject expressing two separate processes, however, requires a plural verb.

 But <u>preventing</u> hacking and <u>identifying</u> fake accounts *continues* to be more art than science. (*New York Times*)

Fifth, if *A* and *B* are nouns that together form the name of a dish (such as *pork and sauerkraut* or *spaghetti and sea urchin*), choose a singular verb.

Sixth, if the *A and B* construction is preceded by the adjective *each* or *every*, a singular verb is required.

 ...each <u>physician</u> and <u>patient</u> *are* different.... (ehow.com)

6 Neither he nor she agree on whether this sentence is correct.

We often get into mischief when we write sentences whose subjects take the form *A or B*, *A nor B*, *either A or B*, or *neither A nor B*. We too easily forget that *or* and the fancier-sounding word *nor* are not synonymous with *and*.

 Even the most "wonderfully told tale" of unraveling family life and marital infidelity, she argues, doesn't deliver the jolt we get when Emma Bovary or Anna Karenina *risk* it all for love. (*New Republic*)

 ...neither the copy nor the original *appear* to survive. (*Elizabeth Bishop and* The New Yorker [Farrar, Straus and Giroux], edited by Joelle Biele)

We need to be mindful that when we write *A or B*, we mean one or the other, not both. The same is true of subjects in the variant forms *A nor B*, *either A or B*, and *neither A nor B*. In such formations, *A* and *B* are alternatives. Let's call such formations alternative-compound subjects.

The rule that guides us to the correct verb when the subject is an alternative compound is simple: the verb is conjugated to agree with the *B* element, the part of the subject closer to the verb. If the *B* element is singular, the verb needs to be singular; if the *B* element is plural, the verb needs to be plural.

In the pair of erroneous specimens above, the italicized verbs must be singularized. Often, though, one or more nouns (or pronouns) appearing later in such a sentence must be singularized as well.

 ...a horsey laugh or a misused salad fork are the disqualifying marks of a peasant. (*Vanity Fair*)

 ...a horsey laugh or a misused salad fork is the disqualifying mark....

Sometimes it just makes more sense to replace *or* with *and* if the sentence will sound better that way.

 The Nazi Captain Blicero in *Gravity's Rainbow*, or the ruthless financier Scarsdale Vibe in *Against the Day*, are not truly frightening figures.... (*How Fiction Works* [Farrar, Straus and Giroux], by James Wood)

Substitute *and* for *or*, and the sentence will be fine.

7 Arse-Backwards Sentences

In most sentences we write, we position the subject before the verb. That way, we achieve the standard, familiar, and optimally reader-friendly ordering of words. But writers seeking variety in their style occasionally compose a sentence in which the verb precedes the subject. A sentence with that back-to-front arrangement of its two main parts is called an inverted sentence.

Inverted sentences are unusually susceptible to the perils of subject-verb disagreement, because writers often lose track of which noun or pronoun is the subject.

It's easy to forget that any nouns preceding a verb are often the objects of prepositions and do not constitute the subject, as in each of the following sentences (in which the introductory prepositional phrases are underlined, the subject is boldfaced, and the incorrect verb is italicized).

Among the Pop masterpieces on view *are* Robert Rauschenberg's "**Canyon**" (1959), which involves a taxidermy bald eagle and was front-page news when the Sonnabend family donated it to the museum in 2012. (*New Yorker*) [A comma is needed before *in 2012*; see Chapter 70.]

Quick fix: substitute *is* for *are*.

The verb in an inverted sentence with an additive-compound subject (see Chapter 5) can easily be misconjugated.

Among the attractions *is* "**Concerto for Buildings**," a presentation on Greene Street by Mantra Percussion and the students of the Face the Music ensemble, in which four composers (including Paula Matthusen) will employ twenty-four percussionists to play buildings as instruments; "**Exquisite Corpses**," a series of continuous concerts offered at many of the city's cemeteries (including Grant's Tomb and Trinity Wall Street); and "**Sousapalooza**," a happening at Bryant Park's Upper Terrace.... (*New Yorker*)

Quick fix: substitute *are* for *is*.

8 There, there.

Writers who start a clause with the word *there* sometimes choose a singular verb when a plural verb is required. You never want to mistake the word *there* for a subject. The subject of a clause beginning with *there* will always be found later in the phrasing. In such clauses, whose ordering of the subject and the verb is inverted, *there* is nothing more than a structural support. (Grammarians call it an expletive.)

In the excerpt below, the subject is underlined. The incorrect verb, *is*, is contracted in *there's*. The quickest fix is to substitute *there are* for *there's*.

...there's about 75 million Catholics in America.... (*Wall Street Journal*)

Things are more flexible, though, when the subject of a clause beginning with *there* is an additive-compound subject (see Chapter 5). A plural verb is certainly correct (the nouns that together form the subject of each of the sentences below are underlined).

There are a young woman, a middle-aged man, and a woman in her late sixties waiting outside.

It's permissible, though, to use a singular verb in such sentences as well.

 There is a <u>bracelet</u>, a <u>necklace</u>, and a single <u>earring</u>.

A singular verb is acceptable even if one or more plural elements follow one or more singular elements in an additive-compound subject.

 There was an upright <u>piano</u>, three <u>chairs</u>, and a <u>cot</u>.

If all of the nouns in the additive-compound subject are plural, however, the verb must be plural.

 There's the solitary <u>households</u> we're supposed to adapt to, and the shifting <u>workplaces</u> we're being asked to accept. (*Lonely: A Memoir* [Harper], by Emily White)

Quick fix: substitute *There are* for *There's*.

9 Adjectival dependent clauses are a grammatical construction that lead many writers to commit subject-verb agreement errors, like the one in this sentence.

An adjectival dependent clause is a dependent clause in the same line of work as a single-word adjective: it makes its living by describing a noun. The sentences *She offered a brilliant suggestion* and *She offered a suggestion that was brilliant* each say the same thing, but in the second sentence, *that was brilliant* is a three-word adjectival dependent clause (the subject is *that*, the verb is *was*, and the complement is *brilliant*) accomplishing what the lone word *brilliant* accomplishes in the first sentence. We can't do without adjectival dependent clauses, because the descriptive or elaborative detail we want to pin to a noun is often not reducible to a single word. The only adjectival dependent clauses we need to concern ourselves with here are those beginning with *that* and *which*—words that grammarians call relative pronouns.

The singularity or plurality of the verb following the relative pronoun in such a clause is determined by the singularity or plurality of the antecedent of that pronoun. The antecedent is simply the noun to which the pronoun refers. That noun will be positioned somewhere before the dependent clause, but it won't always be the noun immediately preceding the pronoun.

 Through persistent lobbying, banlieue entrepreneurs have been founding "angel" investment funds, persuading big French companies like AXA Insurance and BNP Paribas to contribute seed money that fuel start-ups ranging from trash removal to taxi fleets. (*New York Times*)

The subject of the adjectival dependent clause *that fuel start-ups ranging from trash removal to taxi fleets* is the relative pronoun *that*, whose antecedent is *money*, a singular noun. The verb in the adjectival dependent clause thus needs to be singularized: *fuels*.

Sometimes the antecedent of the relative pronoun is an additive-compound subject (see Chapter 5).

–11–

 She informs me of her panic disorder and agoraphobia, which has contributed to a bad case of writer's block.... (*New York*)

Quick fix: substitute *have* for *has*.

10 The Lonesome *One*

About one of every five sentences starting off with phrasing such as *About one of every five sentences* or *Only one in five sentences* ends up with the wrong form of the verb—a plural instead of a singular.

 About one in five customers pay cash. (*New York Times*)

 Only about 1 in 20 black women are interracially married. (*Wall Street Journal*)

None of us would write a sentence like *One are absent.* In the sentences above, though, the writers were distracted by the plural object in the prepositional phrase following *one*. Remember that objects of prepositions almost never determine the singularity or plurality of a verb (see Chapter 1). The erroneous sentences above need singular verbs.

Sometimes it's a pronoun, not a verb, that bollixes things up in a sentence beginning with phrasing like *One in every five women.*

 ... only one in ten women said they had experienced love at first sight. (dailymail.co.uk)

The past-tense verb *said* would of course be correct with either a singular or a plural subject, but the plural pronoun *they* clashes with the singular antecedent: *one*. The solution: replace *they* with *she*.

11 Either of these sentences are wrong. Neither of these sentences are correct.

Either and *neither* are indefinite pronouns—pronouns that, unlike personal pronouns (such as *she* or *they*), do not refer to one or more nouns appearing previously in a sentence. There is nothing indefinite, though, about the status of *either* and *neither* as pronouns that are unyieldingly singular in meaning. Only a singular verb, then, will do when *either* or *neither* is the subject. Writers often trip up, however, when *either* or *neither* is followed by a prepositional phrase whose object is plural.

In each example below, the italicized verb is plural when it needs to be singular. The prepositional phrase trailing after *either* or *neither* is underlined.

 ...they had no proof that either <u>of the men</u> *were* involved in any crime. (*New York Times*)

 Neither <u>of these story lines</u> *pass* the straight-face test.... (*New York Times*)

Mentally insert the word *one* after *either* or *neither* in any such sentence, and you'll always be sure to choose the correct form of the verb: *Neither [one] of them is guilty.*

12 To each her own singular verb.

When writing about each of several persons or things, you're singling out one of them for lone consideration. The verb in an *each of the Xs* construction must therefore be singular. If you bear in mind that there's an implied *one* after every *each*, you'll never end up with a plural verb. Ignore any prepositional phrases that follow *each*; the plurality of one or more of the objects of the prepositions may lead you to choose a plural verb. Each of the italicized plural verbs in the following sentences needs to be singularized.

 Each of the three *are* receiving $5,000. (*Wall Street Journal*)

 Each of these works *are* priced at $3 million or under.... (*New York*)

Sometimes, as in the following sentence, in which the error in subject-verb agreement appears in the second half of a compound predicate, *each* can be replaced with a plural pronoun.

 [about four short stories by Elizabeth Bishop] I notice that each appeared in due course in such places as *Harper's Bazaar* and *The New Yorker*, and *were* reprinted in the "Best" collections of the year. (*American Fictions* [Modern Library], by Elizabeth Hardwick)

 I notice that they appeared ... and were reprinted in the annual "Best" collections.

Like *each*, an inherently singular indefinite pronoun, the indefinite pronouns *everybody* and *everyone* always require singular verbs as well. The italicized verb in the next excerpt must be replaced with *was*.

 ... everyone in the theater stayed put well past midnight and *were* "positively limp" by the end. (*Farther and Wilder: The Lost Weekends and Literary Dreams of Charles Jackson* [Knopf], by Blake Bailey)

13 Number-Crunching

When we begin a clause with *a number of* or *the number of*, we sometimes forget that the phrasings aren't interchangeable. We can easily substitute adjectives like *most, many, some,* and *few* for *a number of*, a phrase used when persons or things belonging to a group are being considered separately and severally, not as a mass or a lump sum. But *the number of* is a construction of an entirely different sort: it means *the entire quantity of*. *A number of* requires a plural verb, but *the number of* requires a singular verb.

 ... the number of minutes offered in mobile plans have increased significantly. (*New York Times*)

Quick fix: substitute *has* for *have*.

 A number of studies shows that inquiry learning involves many different cognitive processes.... (from the abstract of a master's-degree thesis)

Quick fix: substitute *show* for *shows*.

We're even more likely to go wrong when *number* appears in an inverted sentence beginning with *there* (see Chapter 8).

 Of course there is a number of reasons why streamers decide to illegally stream live sports coverage.... (forbes.com)

Quick fix: substitute *are* for *is*.

14 The majority rules—or rule?

A majority of the American writerly population chooses a singular verb in a sentence like this. But a majority of American writers choose a plural verb in a sentence like this.

How to explain the difference? Have a look at the object of the preposition in the prepositional phrase following the noun *majority* in each sentence. In the first sentence, the object is the singular noun *population*—and thus a singular verb is required. In the second sentence, the object is the plural noun *writers*—and thus a plural verb is required.

Here we encounter one of the few exceptions to the rule (see Chapter 1) that the object of a preposition has no bearing on whether a verb should be singular or plural. (Another exception is discussed in Chapter 15.)

 Recent polls indicate that a majority of Americans now agrees that same-sex marriage should be legal.... (*New York Times*)

Quick fix: pluralize the verb.

The same principle applies to the noun *minority*: the singularity or plurality of the object of the preposition in the prepositional phrase following *minority* determines whether the verb should be singular or plural.

And what if *majority* or *minority* isn't followed by a prepositional phrase? Ask yourself which prepositional phrase is implied after *majority* or *minority*, and then choose the verb accordingly: *A majority [of the workforce] approves. A majority [of the workers] approve.*

15 Twelve percent of the readership of this book find nothing ungrammatical about this sentence.

That twelve percent of the readership is wrong, though. So is the writer of the following sentence.

 At the show's peak, sixty per cent of the viewing public were watching the series.... (*New Yorker*)

When the subject of a clause is *percent* (or *per cent*, as *The New Yorker* prefers to spell it), the singularity or plurality of the verb is determined by the singularity or plurality of the object of the preposition in the prepositional phrase that follows *percent*. In the excerpt above, the object of the preposition—*public*—is singular, so the verb needs to be singularized. Substitute a plural noun such as *Americans* for *the viewing public*, though, and the plural verb would be correct.

16 More errors like these means more slipshoddiness in print and online.

 Too few workers leads to operational problems. (businessweek.com)

The subject of that slapdash sentence is the plural noun *workers*, yet the writer tosses in the singular verb *leads*. What gives? Simple—the writer is cutting corners and outsourcing some of her work to the reader. The reader is expected to rummage around in her head for an appropriate word or phrase to position at the head of the sentence—not only to ensure that the subject and the verb will agree but also to smooth out the wording. A gerund, such as *having* or *hiring*, would do nicely. The noun *workers* will then function as the object of the gerund, not as the subject of the sentence. But why not spare the reader the trouble? Don't *imply* the subject—spell it out.

 Hiring too few workers leads to operational problems. OR: A shortage of workers leads to operational problems. OR: Short-staffing leads to operational problems.

17 You can be one of the few writers who understands what's wrong with this sentence.

Writers often stumble when composing sentences that include phrasing such as *one of those people who* or *one of the things that*.

 Alzheimer's is one of those cataclysms that seems designed specifically to test the human spirit. (*How We Die: Reflections on Life's Final Chapter* [Knopf], by Sherwin B. Nuland)

There are two ways to understand why a plural, not singular, verb is inevitable in such constructions. The first explanation requires no grammatical terminology at all. Look more closely at the example. A single thing (in this case, a disease) is being placed into a category of things (in this case, the category consists of cataclysms), and a statement is being made not only about Alzheimer's but also about the other members of the category. The verb thus needs to be pluralized so that it embraces all of the members, not just Alzheimer's alone. All of the cataclysms in that category "seem designed specifically to test the human spirit."

The grammatical explanation of why such a sentence calls for a plural verb requires us to recognize that the sentence comprises two clauses—an independent clause (*Alzheimer's is one of those cataclysms*) and an adjectival dependent clause (*that seems designed specifically to test the human spirit*). The subject of the adjectival dependent clause is the relative pronoun *that*. A relative pronoun has an antecedent: a previous noun to which the pronoun refers. In the sentence under examination, *that* is substituting for the plural noun *cataclysms* and therefore cannot manage without a plural verb.

18 My family is recovering from my bad grammar. No, wait. My family *are* recovering from my bad grammar?

Family belongs to a troublous subset of nouns called collective nouns. (Among the many others are *crew, audience, crowd, team, staff, group,* and *trio.*) A collective noun (1) names a pair or a group of people but (2) does not end in *s* or *es*.

Collective nouns are exasperating because every time you use one, you must decide whether to interpret it in a singular sense or in a plural sense. You otherwise won't know whether the noun needs a singular verb or a plural one. Two rules will guide you.

First, if you want to emphasize the group as a single entity with a common goal or viewpoint, choose a singular verb (*Her band is performing tonight*).

Second, if you want to emphasize the group as a collection of individuals differing in their opinions and objectives, choose a plural verb (*Her band are butting heads over possible titles for the new album*).

Things get complicated, though, as soon as a pronoun referring back to the collective noun enters the picture. If you've decided on a singular verb for the collective noun, the pronoun must also be singular. If you've chosen a plural verb, the pronoun must be plural. You therefore have to settle on either a singular or a plural interpretation of the collective noun and then be consistent with both verbs and pronouns.

It's unbecoming, even unnatural, for a collective noun to behave as if it's both singular and plural—especially within the bounds of a single sentence. In the following excerpts, the collective nouns are italicized, the problematic verbs are underlined, and the pronouns with collective nouns as their antecedents are boldfaced.

In an unconscious gesture of solidarity, Aronofsky's *team* often <u>adopts</u> his current hair style—recently a shaved head and a thick beard—as if someone were mass-grooming **them** using the magnetic Wooly Willy game. (*New Yorker*)

Around the time [Robert] Frost wrote those words, his *family* <u>was</u> living what he termed **their** "mildly literary life" in a London suburb.... (*New Yorker*)

In each sentence, a singular verb clashes with a plural pronoun. Ideally, the plural interpretation, emphasizing individual members, should prevail here—so the verbs must be converted to their plural forms. (If a writer wants to make a strong case for a singular interpretation of the second sentence, however, the verb and the pronoun must both be singular.)

The examples thus far have been single sentences. But errors in handling collective nouns often do not arise until a writer has moved from one sentence to the next.

The dining room *staff* <u>makes</u> a great show of brisk efficiency. They <u>wear</u> white coats and neckties.... (*New York Times*)

Since the staff are not performing their duties in lockstep, the plural interpretation is needed throughout. (A hyphen must unite *dining* and *room*; see Chapter 86.)

The mismanagement of collective nouns is rampant in the sections of newspapers and magazines listing upcoming performances by musical groups, as well as in reviews. A writer sometimes shifts from the singular to the plural and then back to the singular—all within a single clause.

... the *band* <u>drives</u> a biodiesel-fuelled tour bus, <u>plants</u> trees to offset **their** carbon-dioxide output, and <u>packages</u> **its** CDs using entirely postconsumer recycled materials. (*New Yorker*)

19 Couples in Crisis

The noun *couple*, despite our tending to think of it as denoting two persons united into an indivisible whole, almost always requires a plural verb. Sentences in which *couple* appears, in fact, usually emphasize the two individuals of which the couple is (or once was) composed: *The couple are getting engaged. The couple are separating. The couple are thinking about reuniting.*

Only when the two partners are functioning together as a single entity is the singular verb appropriate: *The couple is moving to Houston. The couple is honeymooning in Mexico.* In each of the following excerpts, however, the writer chose a singular verb when only the plural interpretation is reasonable.

In the first, the plural pronoun *their* is the giveaway that a plural verb is needed.

The couple lives in a Houston high-rise with a live-in nanny for their daughters.... (*Wall Street Journal*)

The giveaway in the next example is the reciprocal pronoun *each other's*.

... the couple falls into each other's arms in the last scene. (*New York Times*)

In the following example, the giveaway is the phrase *one of them*.

... a third couple is advised to try role-playing, although one of them finds it far too consuming to be bothered with its erotic side. (*New Yorker*)

What's true of *couple* applies as well to the nouns *pair* and *duo*.

This mismatched pair has only one thing in common: They've both got less than a year left. (*New York Observer*)

Quick fix: substitute *have* for *has*.

Couple, pair, and *duo,* in short, are collective nouns and must be treated as such (see Chapter 18).

Placement Services

20 Flailing Phrases

Grammarians reserve the term *dangling modifier* for a descriptive phrase flailing and flapping about within a sentence in a futile search for a noun or a pronoun it might fittingly describe. The tragedy is that the sentence lacks any noun or pronoun to which the phrase can fasten itself in a secure, conclusive way. The most that the hapless descriptive phrase can manage is cozying up to the nearest available noun or pronoun, but the two of them always turn out to be incompatible and make no sense together at all. In fact, they often make for a laughable match.

 Flying from Boston to New York, my habit is to take a seat on the right-hand side of the plane.... (*New Yorker*)

Maybe a hobbit could make the flight from Beantown to the Big Apple, but could a habit?

The *New Yorker* sentence reveals the irreality common to many sentences incapacitated by a dangling modifier: human activity is reportedly taking place, but there's nobody present to perform it or even witness it. Such sentences are eerily *unpeopled.* To set things right, you need to usher into the sentence a member of the human race functioning either as an actor or as a perceiver. There are two easy ways to do that—two methods that will work for most dangling modifiers.

The first is to expand the descriptive phrase into an adverbial dependent clause—the sort of dependent clause that begins with a subordinating conjunction (a word such as *although, while,* or *because*) and that includes both a subject (in this case, of course, the subject had better well have a pulse) and a verb.

 When I am flying from Boston to New York, my habit is to take a seat on the right-hand side of the plane....

The other way to correct the error is to let the descriptive phrase alone and do some major reconstructive work on the independent clause. You'll need to start the new independent clause with a subject logically compatible with the descriptive phrase at the outset of the sentence.

 Flying from Boston to New York, I habitually take a seat on the right-hand side of the plane....

Dangling modifiers also derange sentences in which the noun that the writer has intended to serve as the subject of the independent clause is locked away inside a possessive adjective—an adjective formed either by the combination of a singular noun, an apostrophe, and the letter *s*, or by the combination of a plural noun ending in *s* and an apostrophe. (Or the intended subject might have morphed itself unhelpfully into a possessive pronoun, such as *her* or *their*.) The possessive adjective is then followed by a noun with which the introductory descriptive phrase is logically unsuited.

 [from a review of a photographer's work] Wearing outsized heads, the figures' cloying cuteness is subverted by sexy outfits: mermaids, miniskirts, latex. (*New Yorker*)

The writer wanted *figures* to serve as the subject, but that noun is stranded helplessly in the possessive adjective *figures'*. The result is that *cuteness* is forced against its will into the role of subject.

 The cloying cuteness of the figures, who wear outsized heads, is subverted by sexy outfits.... OR: Wearing outsized heads, the figures subvert their cloying cuteness by having donned sexy outfits.... [Some readers, of course, might still challenge the logic of the phrasing of the series that follows the colon; substituting *mermaid suits* for *mermaids* would help.]

Dangling modifiers often arise from a writer's desire to be as concise as possible at any cost, as in this sentence from an article about a dancer who goes by the name Storyboard P:

 Growing up, Storyboard's best friend was a kid named Nelson Adolphus, who wanted to be a scientist. (*New Yorker*)

The two-word participial phrase *growing up* is intended to modify *Storyboard*, but *Storyboard* has been demoted from nounal status to adjectival status by dint of the clipped-on apostrophe and *s*. The participial phrase ends up modifying *friend*—at odds with the writer's purpose. If we can assume that the best-friendship was reciprocated by Adolphus, it's possible to rework the seventeen-word sentence without lengthening it by as much as a single word.

 Growing up, Storyboard was best friends with Nelson Adolphus, a kid who wanted to be a scientist.

Another option, of course, is to enlarge the participial phrase into a dependent clause, thereby adding three words to the sentence.

 When Storyboard was growing up, his best friend was a kid named Nelson Adolphus, who wanted to be a scientist.

Most dangling modifiers take the form of participial phrases, but nonparticipial adjectival phrases can flail as well.

 Seven years in the making, the sculpture's strange balance of power and vulnerability, stillness and emotion, carries more than a hint of the complex relationship between Ray and Pastor. (*New Yorker*)

 The sculpture was seven years in the making, and its strange balance of power and vulnerability, stillness and emotion, carries more than a hint of the complex relationship....

A dangling modifier most often appears at the start of a sentence, but it might also show up midway.

 One evening Ed Landberg heard Pauline broadcasting on KPFA, and after telephoning to compliment her on the program, they arranged to meet. (*Pauline Kael: A Life in the Dark* [Viking], by Brian Kellow)

 One evening, Ed Landberg heard Pauline broadcasting on KPFA, and after he telephoned to compliment her on the program, they arranged to meet.

Finally, a dangling modifier might appear at the end of a sentence.

 Yet there is no further mention [in the book] of anything done by Straus that can be called editing, leaving to others in the firm the "care and feeding" of chosen FSG authors. (*New Republic*)

 Yet there is no further mention of anything Straus did that can be called editing, the "care and feeding" of chosen FSG authors having been left to others in the firm. OR: Yet there is no further mention of anything Straus did that can be called editing, because the "care and feeding" of chosen FSG authors was left to others in the firm.

21 Based on the title of this chapter, I still have a lot to learn.

Based on something a friend told me, my decision not to move to Brooklyn seems reasonable; and based on what I remember of my childhood fears of the Goodyear blimp, my aversion to attending air shows makes perfect sense. So far, so good. But if I then go ahead and say that based on what I've heard about the new Belle and Sebastian CD, I don't think I'll buy it, my grammar, syntax, and logic are shot to hell.

Why? It's simple, or at least it should be. If I'm going to start a sentence with *based on X*, then the comma has to be followed by a subject that names whatever it is that *X* is the basis of. The subject cannot get away with naming something for which *X* can't serve as the foundation. In the first two examples in the paragraph above, a decision is based on something a friend told me, and an aversion is based on something I remember. But in the third example, *I* am based on what I've heard about a CD. I can be accused of many things, but being based on something I've heard is not one of them.

A sentence starting with *based on* can easily go haywire.

 Based on the album and subsequent live performances, the energy level of the band hasn't abated one bit.... (*New Yorker*)

This sentence tells the reader that the energy level of a band is based on an album and live performances—and not, say, on stamina resulting from grueling rehearsals, strenuous exercise, and a sound diet. Repairing such a construction usually involves demolishing the *based on* phrasing and building part of the sentence anew.

The album and subsequent live performances prove that the energy level of the band hasn't abated....

 Trainum searched for more evidence, and got the logbook of the shelter where Kimberly had been staying. Based on when she had signed in and out, he didn't see how Kimberly could have taken part in the murder—she'd been inside the shelter during the critical times. (*New Yorker*)

 After noting when she had signed in and out, he didn't see how Kimberly could have taken part in the murder....

 Based on Breivik's political rhetoric and his self-understanding, and also on his chosen targets—Regjeringskvartalet and the ruling party's youth organization—it is natural to draw a comparison between his act and the 1995 bombing in Oklahoma City.... (*New Yorker*) [The sentence is compromised as well by a multitasking dash; see Chapter 84.]

 Because of Breivik's political rhetoric and his self-understanding, as well as his chosen targets....

22 In the Wrong Place at the Wrong Time

In the crowd of words in a sentence, it's easy for a descriptive word or word-group to get separated from the word it wants to describe. The inevitable fate of the word or word-group that wanders off is that it ends up in the company of another word, a word with which it simply doesn't belong. The errant word or word-group tries its best to work its descriptive powers on its new companion, and what happens next is sometimes comical but more often just plain annoying. Either way, the intended meaning of the sentence gets distorted, and everybody loses.

The descriptive word or word-group that has lost its place in a sentence is called a misplaced modifier. The single-word modifiers most frequently misplaced are *only, merely, just,* and *not*. If the misplaced modifier is a word-group, it can be a prepositional phrase, a participial phrase, an adjectival dependent clause, or an adverbial dependent clause.

Whenever a modifier isn't positioned right next to the word it's intended to describe, you need to bring the two together. Luckily, that's not difficult to do. It's often just a matter of nudging the misplaced modifier either forward or backward in the sentence so that it ends up beside the word it wants to modify. (Some further but minor reconstruction of the sentence is occasionally needed as well.)

The misplaced modifier in each of the following excerpts is underlined and takes the form of a phrase or a dependent clause.

 Scientists have been trying to determine why people need sleep <u>for more than 100 years</u>. (*New York Times*)

 For more than a hundred years, scientists have been trying to determine why people need sleep.

 According to Lorraine C. Minnite, a scholar of voter fraud at Columbia University, records show that only twenty-four people were convicted of or pleaded guilty to illegal voting between 2002 and 2005, an average of eight people a year. (*Common Nonsense: Glenn Beck and the Triumph of Ignorance* [Wiley], by Alexander Zaitchik)

 According to Lorraine C. Minnite, a Columbia University scholar of voter fraud.... OR: According to Lorraine C. Minnite, a scholar who researches voter fraud and who teaches at Columbia University....

 Enter Matt Cohen, whose company, Kidfresh, sells frozen meals for children that are lower in fat and sodium and higher in some nutritional elements like fiber. (*New York Times*)

 Enter Matt Cohen, whose company, Kidfresh, sells child-friendly frozen meals that are lower in fat and sodium....

Misplaced single-word modifiers are easily resituated in their sentences.

 [from an article about a drum major's hazing-related death] The marching band has been suspended from performing indefinitely. (*New York Times*)

The writer surely doesn't mean that the band is now prohibited from subjecting audiences to concerts that seem as if they'll never end.

 The marching band has been indefinitely suspended from performing. OR: Until further investigation, the marching band has been suspended from performing.

Many contemporary writers and editors, though, think that it's often fine to leave a misplaced single-word modifier right where it has landed in a sentence. They would argue that only a fusspot would see any reason to relocate the modifiers *just* and *only* in the sentences below. They would claim that any reader will instantly understand what each sentence is intended to mean. Grammatically conservative writers and editors, though, would insist on repositioning each single-word modifier as suggested in the bracketed and italicized rephrasing following each sentence.

 Lululemon Athletica Inc.'s yoga pants aren't just worn in the gym anymore. (*Wall Street Journal*) [*aren't worn just in the gym anymore*]

 She also published enough short stories to fill a couple of books, but people who only wrote fiction were not given offices. (*Ornament and Silence: Essays on Women's Lives* [Knopf], by Kennedy Fraser) [*but people who wrote only fiction were not given offices*]

It's up to you to decide whether to achieve the precision that's ensured by placing *only* or any similar one-word modifier directly in front of the word it's intended to modify. But if you prefer the loose, conversational-sounding placement, be forewarned that the resulting sentences can easily invite misinterpretation. What, for instance, is a reader expected to make of the sentence *I'll only call you after ten o'clock*? The writer might well mean that *I won't be calling you before ten,* but a reader might construe the sentence as saying *The only way I'll get in touch with you after ten is by phone; that is, I won't be texting you, or e-mailing you, or instant-messaging you, or communicating with you in any other way after ten o'clock.*

23 The Laggard Modifier

A new form of inelegance has arrived on our pages and screens: a modifier that is neither misplaced to the detriment of the writer's meaning (see Chapter 22) nor dangling illogically and ungrammatically (see Chapter 20). It nonetheless throws the sentence into some disarray; even inattentive readers are likely to register that something is subtly off. This error is what we might call a laggard modifier—one that shows up a little too late in the sentence. It usually takes the form of a phrase, often beginning with the preposition *like* or the participle *including,* but sometimes it can be a dependent clause. A laggard modifier typically enriches a sentence by providing examples (often in a pair or in a list). But its peculiar placement jars the reader, who often can't resist the temptation to guide the modifier backward in the sentence, repositioning it so that it follows the word (usually a noun) or the word-group (usually an adjectival phrase or adjectival dependent clause) that it's intended to modify.

The laggard modifiers have been underscored in the following excerpts.

The hotel has high-tech features meant to keep prices low and customers happy <u>like automated check-in kiosks and a "Yobot," or robotic luggage concierge</u>. (*New York Times*)

The hotel has high-tech features—like automated check-in kiosks and a "Yobot," or robotic luggage concierge—meant to keep prices low. . . .

But many of the adults I spoke to in Steubenville feigned ignorance about the rape, <u>including the high school's principal and football coach</u>, or blamed the victim for what happened. (*New York Times*)

But many of the adults I spoke to in Steubenville, including the high school's principal and its football coach, feigned ignorance about the rape. . . .

24 Writers who commit this error sometimes feel bad about it.

If you think that this is going to be a chapter telling you that the phrase *feel bad* in the title should be replaced with *feel badly,* I'm sorry, because nowhere in this book will such wrongheaded advice be dispensed. (One should feel bad about writing badly, but feeling badly would mean there is something wrong with one's sense of touch.) The trouble with the phrasing of the title is the heedless positioning of the adverb *sometimes.* Thanks to the writer's carelessness, the sentence is saying two conflicting things at once, and the alert reader will wonder which of the two possible meanings is the one the writer intended. A statement susceptible to two or more clashing interpretations is said to be ambiguous.

Beware of any modifier—either a single-word adverb, like *sometimes,* or an adverbial phrase—that displays itself teasingly and suggestively between two verbs or between a verb and a verbal (an infinitive, a gerund, or a participle). The result is that a reader won't know which one of the two verbal forms the modifier belongs to. In the sentence *Writers who commit this error sometimes feel bad about it,* the adverb *sometimes* is simultaneously modifying *commit* and *feel*. But the adverb needs to pledge itself to one verb or the other—it can't carry on with both.

The problem can be resolved by sliding the adverb around in the sentence until it clicks into place and thereby ensures that the statement's meaning is in accord with the writer's intention.

 Writers who sometimes commit this error feel bad about it. [The adverb is unambiguously modifying *commit;* the meaning is that the error is committed only occasionally.]

 Writers who commit this error feel bad about it sometimes. [The adverb is unambiguously modifying *feel;* the meaning is that writers don't always feel bad about having committed the error. The same meaning would be expressed by *Sometimes writers who commit this error feel bad about it.*]

 Women who have been assaulted often worry, with reason, about being victimized a second time in court. (*New York Times*)

The positioning of *often* between *assaulted* and *worry* leaves a reader confused, if only for a millisecond, about whether the sentence means *Women who have often been assaulted worry, with reason, about being victimized a second time in court* or *Women who have been assaulted worry, often with reason, about being victimized a second time in court.* The writer most likely intended to express what the latter of those revisions states unmisleadingly.

A writer should avoid even the remotest possibility that a reader might register a modifier as ambiguous.

 Reading this [tale] to my daughter recently, for the first time in thirty-five years, I was instantly returned, by the talismanic activity of that "cherry-coloured twist," to a memory of my mother reading it to me. (*How Fiction Works* [Farrar, Straus and Giroux], by James Wood)

The writer surely doesn't want readers to entertain the possibility that he has recently read a story aloud to a daughter who is now in early middle age, but it's awfully easy to form that impression.

 As I was reading this to my daughter recently, the talismanic activity of that "cherry-coloured twist" instantly returned me, for the first time in thirty-five years, to a memory of my mother reading the story to me.

25 Don't leave your adverbs out in the cold.

If you're going to use a single-word adverb to modify a verb phrase (a phrase, such as *had gone*, that consists of at least one helping, or auxiliary, verb and a main verb), there's something you ought to know. The snuggest place for that adverb is precisely to the right of the helping verb, not to the left of it and not to the right of the main verb.

There's a widespread resistance, though, to splitting the verb phrase. It seems to be a side effect of the fear of splitting an infinitive (see Chapter 52), but the two kinds of splits are entirely unrelated. So please do try to find the warmest spot for your adverbs.

 ...there was no doubt that this audience had enjoyed mightily what it had just seen.... (*New York Times*)

 ...this audience had mightily enjoyed what it had just seen....

 Twenty-five of the 300 films that were shot ultimately were chosen to be part of the new campaign. (*New York Times*)

 Twenty-five of the three hundred films that were shot were ultimately chosen to be part of the new campaign.

When a verb phrase consists of two helping verbs and a main verb, the usual advice is to position the adverb after the first helping verb. In the second sentence of the following excerpt, though, some readers are likely to feel that the right place for *probably* is after *have* and that the right place for *fervently* is after *praying*.

 Is there a patron saint of befuddled theatergoers? Had I known of one, I would probably have been fervently praying at intervals throughout "The Patron Saint of Sea Monsters," a wayward, Gothic comedy-drama.... (*New York Times*)

Let your ear—or your intuition—guide you in choosing where an adverb might be ensconced for maximum comfort.

Even when helping verbs are out of the picture, adverbs sometimes end up in the most precarious positions (see also Chapter 22). Reading a sentence aloud can help you find a more inviting place for the adverb to settle down.

 But while she always meant to treat kindly her adorable "Scramdoodle," she could turn on a dime too, and then her moods became possessive. (*Bobbed Hair and Bathtub Gin* [Harcourt], by Marion Meade)

 ...she always meant to treat her adorable "Scramdoodle" kindly....

Finally, a clumsily situated adverb can distort the writer's intended meaning (see Chapter 22).

 [quoted in an article about a company about to eliminate many positions] "We do not make plans that may impact our employees lightly...." (*New York Times*)

"Making plans that may impact our employees is not something we take lightly...."

26 The Overreaching Modifier

The next time you find yourself setting out words or word-groups in a pair or in a series, you might want to be especially alert if you're positioning in front of the first item a modifier that you want to apply to that item and that item alone. It may well turn out that the modifier has other things in mind. A modifier is sometimes too ambitious—not just for its own good but for the good of the entire sentence in which it appears. Instead of confining its descriptive or limital powers to the word that immediately follows it, the modifier can throw its weight forward in the sentence so that the modifier does its job on the next available word as well, even when that word was intended to remain unmodified. The result is a sentence whose meaning conflicts with the meaning intended by the writer.

 At Indiana University Health, a large health system, employees who do not smoke and achieve a certain body mass index, or B.M.I., can receive up to $720 a year off the cost of their insurance. (*New York Times*)

The adverb *not* is throwing its weight around and spreading its influence far forward in the sentence—and thus applying itself not only to *smoke* but to *achieve* as well.

 ... employees who do not smoke and who achieve a certain body-mass index, or B.M.I., can receive up to $720 a year off the cost....

27 The Unhinged Appositive

If you're going to start a sentence with a phrase like *A graduate of Brooklyn College* or *A woman in early middle age*, consider yourself safe if the very next thing you do is type a verb or a verb phrase: *is flourishing* would work nicely enough. But if, instead, you press the comma key, be careful. If you follow the comma with a person's name or a subjective pronoun such as *she* (see Chapter 30), you're home free. If you follow that comma with a possessive pronoun or a possessive noun, though, your sentence is a goner. You'll end up with a miscreation like *A graduate of Brooklyn College, her enthusiasm is contagious* or *A woman in early middle age, Fionella's brilliance is the envy of her colleagues.*

But you won't be alone.

 A natural blonde, her dyed red hair was pulled back tight against her forehead. (*New York Observer*)

 The adopted son of a levee engineer, his youth was spent in Memphis and the Ozarks.... (*New Republic*)

So what exactly is the matter?

Each of the sentences begins with a phrase that grammarians call an appositive—a noun phrase that volunteers information about another noun. An appositive usually follows the noun: in the sentence *Jana, a renowned botanist, moved to Austin*, the appositive is *a renowned botanist*. The noun *Jana* and the phrase *a renowned botanist* make perfect sense together.

But when writers decide to situate an appositive like *a renowned botanist* at the outset of a sentence, they sometimes forget that the appositive, by its very nature, is providing an alternative name or designation for a *person*—a person who hasn't yet made her official entrance into the sentence. So the only possible subject of the sentence's independent clause (the word-group that will follow the comma) is going to have to be a noun (or a pronoun) that in one way or another functions as a name for her—and not a noun that names one of her attributes.

In other words, the introductory appositive and the subject of the independent clause must be equivalent in meaning. An equal sign should be implied between them. But a graduate of Brooklyn College obviously can't equal enthusiasm, and a woman in early middle age can't equal brilliance, though that's what the two sentences closing the first paragraph of this chapter have fatuously declared.

To repair such sentences, you'll need to reconstruct the independent clause so that it begins with a subject to which the appositive can be securely hinged.

 A natural blonde, she wears her dyed-red hair pulled back tight....

 The adopted son of a levee engineer, he spent his youth in Memphis and the Ozarks....

Unhinged appositives do not limit their illogic to sentences about people.

 A venomous and ill-disguised burlesque of prep school life that received blistering reviews, the book's reception precipitated Burns's return to Italy.... (*New York Times*)

 A venomous and ill-disguised burlesque of prep-school life, the book received blistering reviews that precipitated Burns's return to Italy....

Finally, an unhinged appositive sometimes shows up in the middle or at the end of a sentence.

 Vilar had subsequently paid for the young man's college and medical-school education—one of about thirty students he had put through college. (*New Yorker*)

 Vilar had subsequently covered the college and medical-school expenses for the young man—one of about thirty students he had put through college.

28 The Mispositioned Appositive

An appositive—a noun or a noun phrase providing information about another noun—should settle down right next to the noun it's related to, as in the sentence you're now reading: the phrasing set off with dashes is the appositive, and *appositive* is the noun it's spilling some revealing beans about.

A well-behaved appositive never leaves the side of its companionate noun. Many writers, though, are intent on breaking up the pair and putting some painful distance between the two. The result is that a reader sometimes can't immediately recognize that the noun and the appositive are in fact halves of a whole.

 Wodehouse was among the best-paid and best-loved writers in the world during the 1930s, a British institution, and he could afford to have a sense of humor about critics. (*New York Times*)

The appositive, *a British institution*, should be positioned after *Wodehouse*.

 Wodehouse, a British institution, was among the best-paid and best-loved writers....

In some sentences, it might take more than a simple repositioning to get things right.

 A veritable Pittsburgh legend, hundreds upon hundreds of soft pretzels are prepared at The Pretzel Shop by hand daily.... (*Moon Pittsburgh* [Moon Handbooks], by Dan Eldridge)

 Every day, hundreds upon hundreds of soft pretzels are prepared by hand at the Pretzel Shop, a veritable Pittsburgh legend....

Pronouns Are Not for Amateurs

29 They is out of their mind.

The pronoun-usage error most likely to drive finicky readers crazy is the use of the plural pronouns *they, them,* and *their* to refer back to singular nouns or pronouns.

 The average adolescent sends almost two thousand text messages a month. They contact their friends more by text than by phone or e-mail or instant-message or even face-to-face conversations. (*New Yorker*)

Those who defend using *they, them,* and *their* with singular antecedents insist that substituting the politically correct and gender-inclusive pronominal pairs *he or she, him or her,* and *his or her* ultimately clutters a sentence. No argument there. But the fact that the English language lacks a single-word gender-neutral third-person singular pronoun doesn't mean that we should blur the distinction between singularity and plurality.

What to do instead? The standard suggestions to rehabilitate a sentence such as *A shopper gets impatient while they wait in line* are these: (1) pluralize the antecedent (and its verb) so that the plural pronoun is correct (*Shoppers get impatient while they wait in line*); (2) switch the point of view of the sentence from the third-person to the second-person (*You get impatient while you wait in line*); (3) resort to the tiresome and wordy yet undeniably fair-play binary *he or she, him or her,* and *his or her*—unless such a pair is needed more than once in a sentence (*A shopper gets impatient while he or she waits in line*); or (4) rewrite the sentence so that it no longer even requires a pronoun (*A shopper gets impatient while waiting in line*). Writers often overlook the fourth option.

Any of those four tactics will appease picky readers—and, what, after all, is gained by alienating them? There's another way out, though. With women's ascendancy in the educational world and in the workplace, not to mention the fact that women outnumber men, why not adopt *she* and *her* as the default, go-to pronouns for any sentence about a representative but unspecified human being? Such usage would make for cleaner, crisper prose. Many writers have already made the shift, and the increasing use of *she* and *her* to refer to a representative person in a context where sex is irrelevant has begun to look and sound natural, even inevitable, as our world continues to evolve.

 As [George] Saunders told me, "A work of art is something produced by a person, but is not that person—it is of her, but is not her. . . . That's why she writes: to try and briefly be more than she truly is." (*New York Times*)

Whichever tack you take, though, be sure not to mix singular pronouns with plural pronouns.

 Sales is the activity of making another person buy something he or she didn't know they wanted. (*Wall Street Journal*)

Be both correct and consistent within a passage when you are referring to an unparticularized person. And don't get so obsessed with avoiding the misuse of *they, them,* and *their* that you end up using a singular pronoun to refer back to a plural antecedent, as in the following sentence (the writer might have been thrown off by the indefinite pronoun *one*).

 There aren't many directors one can identify simply by looking at a brief clip of his or her work. (*Wall Street Journal*)

Finally, when you're writing about a representative member of a particular subgroup of people, readers may find it awkward or confusing if you abruptly switch from pronouns signifying one sex to those signifying the other, especially within a single paragraph.

 Never touch a disabled guest's wheelchair, which is no different from touching the guest herself. Never address a disabled guest's aide and ignore the guest; address the aide and the guest, bending down, if need be, to make sure the guest knows you're aware of his existence. (*Shoptimism: Why the American Consumer Will Keep On Buying No Matter What* [Free Press], by Lee Eisenberg)

Quick fix: in the second sentence, substitute *her* for *his*.

Pronominal complications arising from the writer's choice of an alternative-compound subject requiring a singular verb (see Chapter 6) are often best resolved by recasting the sentence.

 …neither Moss nor Bishop discuss their personal lives. (*Elizabeth Bishop and* The New Yorker [Farrar, Straus and Giroux], edited by Joelle Biele)

Quick fix: Moss and Bishop never discuss their personal lives.

Errors caused by using plural pronouns with singular antecedents also appear in sentences in which the antecedent is a noun denoting something inanimate.

 Children receive a check for fifty kidzos upon arriving at KidZania, and can supplement that with the "salary" they earn for participating in an activity. The most popular of them, like training to be a pilot on a simplified flight simulator, are not as remunerative as the less popular, like being a dentist. (*New Yorker*)

The antecedent of *them* is the singular noun *activity*. The quickest fix is to substitute *activities* for *an activity* in the first sentence and leave the second sentence alone.

Finally, avoid using the singular pronoun *this* or *that* when the antecedent is plural.

 …her pay and her pension benefits were less than that of her predecessor.… (*New York Times*)

Quick fix: …her pay and her pension benefits were less than those of her predecessor.…

30 We are obsessed with grammar, her and me. Or should it be *she and I?*

The subjective personal pronouns (*I, we, she, he,* and *they*) and their objective counterparts (*me, us, her, him,* and *them*) are rarely misused in print, so only a quick recital of the rules is needed here. (We don't need to worry about the pronoun *you,* which functions as both a subjective and an objective pronoun. The subjective *who* and *whoever* and the objective *whom* and *whomever,* though, are a different story altogether, and the rules governing their use are discussed in Chapter 33.)

Subjective pronouns serve as subjects of clauses (*She and they have arrived*); as subjects of implied verbs (*She is smarter than I* [see Chapter 31]); in the position before appositives in clauses (*We chefs are a fussy bunch*); in appositives following the subjects of clauses (*The new neighbors—she and two daughters—are friendly*); and as complements of linking (or equational) verbs when the complements are followed by an adjectival dependent clause (*It was she who e-mailed the staff*). A subjective pronoun functioning as the complement of a linking verb when no adjectival dependent clause follows (*The winner is she*) now sounds pretentious to many readers, so an objective pronoun is often chosen instead. Finally, a pronoun serving as the complement of the infinitive *to be* in an infinitive phrase consisting of *to be* followed by a pronoun must be in subjective form. But a sentence with that sort of construction will inevitably sound wrong to some readers, so it's usually better to rework the phrasing.

 Increasingly, though, the subject seemed to be him, not her. (*New York Times*)

 …the subject seemed to be he, not she. OR:…he, not she, seemed to be the subject.

Objective pronouns serve as direct objects of transitive verbs (*I texted her*); as indirect objects of transitive verbs (*She gave him and me a reprimand*); and as direct objects of gerunds (*She wouldn't accept money for driving us to the station*), of participles (*The person recommending her is my mother*), and of infinitives (*The company wants to hire her*). Objective pronouns also serve as objects of prepositions (*He dedicated the book to her*); before appositives functioning as objects (*She blamed us interns*); in appositives following objects (*The coach congratulated the new members—her and me*); and as direct objects of implied verbs in elliptical dependent clauses (*She likes her brother more than me* [that is, *She likes her brother more than she likes me*]).

Objective pronouns are also used in a kind of sentence that appears only rarely these days—a sentence in which a pronoun functions as the complement of the infinitive *to be* in an infinitive clause (*We found the culprit to be him*). And strange as it might sound, any pronoun serving as the subject of an infinitive clause must be in objective form as well (*We found him to be the culprit*). Of course, the strange-sounding parenthesized sentences in this paragraph can easily be rephrased as *We found out that he was the culprit.*

Let's return, then, to the troublesome grammatical construction in the title of this chapter, which involves the rule stating that subjective pronouns are used in an appositive following the subject of a sentence and that objective pronouns are used in an appositive following an object. First, though, a simpler example.

 His assistant, me (they made a little show of calling me his "associate"), sat at a desk in a small annex. (*Between You & Me: Confessions of a Comma Queen* [Norton, first edition], by Mary Norris)

The subjective pronoun *I* is needed in the appositive following the subject, but if *His assistant, I,* or *I, his assistant,* sounds ungraceful to you, refashion the sentence.

 I was his assistant (they made a little show of calling me his "associate") and sat at a desk in a small annex.

And the title of this chapter? It should be *We are obsessed with grammar, she and I.* Those sentence-ending coupled pronouns function as a delayed appositive (see Chapter 28) clarifying whom the writer means by *We,* the subject.

31 You would never write a sentence like this, simply because you are smarter than me.

Knowing which category of pronoun—a subjective pronoun (*I, we, she, he,* or *they*) or an objective pronoun (*me, us, her, him,* or *them*)—should follow *than* (or *as,* for that matter) stumps the most brilliant of writers.

 Instead, most of his energy seems to have been devoted to importing a bed into the studio so that his wife, more seriously injured than him in their Scottish car-crash at the end of June, could survey proceedings and lend him moral support. (*Revolution in the Head: The Beatles' Records and the Sixties* [Henry Holt], by Ian MacDonald)

 A handful of other hopefuls also waited to be interviewed, including a huge guy, Ali G'd to the max, far more muscular than me.... (*Shoptimism: Why the American Consumer Will Keep On Buying No Matter What* [Free Press], by Lee Eisenberg)

Some writers, editors, and bystanding grammarians argue in defense of the objective pronoun in such sentences, and others insist on the subjective.

Advocates for the objective pronoun claim that *than* (or *as*) is a preposition, and everybody should know by now that any pronoun serving as the object of a preposition must be an objective pronoun.

Champions of the subjective pronoun insist that *than* (or *as*) is serving as a subordinating conjunction, not as a preposition, and that the pronoun is the subject of an implied verb. In the sentence *She is smarter than I,* the argument goes, the verb *am* makes itself strongly felt despite its invisibility. The phantom *am* fills out the elliptical adverbial dependent clause *than I am.* The objective pronoun *me,* then, would be phosphorescently incorrect.

So on which side of the argument should a writer align herself? The conservative, conscientious choice—and the choice less likely to displease discriminating readers—is to embrace the subjective.

 Dee was two years younger than me, and we had been close.... (*Between You & Me: Confessions of a Comma Queen* [Norton, first edition], by Mary Norris)

Quick fix: substitute *I* for *me*.

32 If I do say so myself ...

It's time to put the pronoun *myself* back in its place. The same goes for its kindred pronouns *yourself, herself, himself, ourselves, yourselves,* and *themselves*—pronouns called compound personal pronouns because of the suffixes *self* and *selves*. These pronouns keep showing up where they don't belong.

 And neither Mr. Jett nor myself would have fallen prey to the so-called Hipster Grifter.... (*New York Times*)

 For the cartoonists, Bob's decision to run humor on the cover was a boon, and many of those who had seldom done covers before, including Bud Handelsman, Bob Mankoff, Roz Chast, Danny Shanahan, and myself, began to appear regularly.... (*The Art of* The New Yorker, *1925-1995* [Knopf], by Lee Lorenz)

In each sentence, *myself* has displaced the correct pronoun—*I* in the first, *me* in the second.

Wishy-washy speakers and writers resort to *myself* whenever they're uncertain about whether *I* or *me* would be correct (see Chapter 30). But *myself,* along with the other compound personal pronouns, has only two legitimate uses.

The first is the emphatic or intensive use. In this use, the pronoun *myself* is not grammatically essential to the sentence but has been set down next to *I* to throw more emphasis on it: *I myself would have quit.*

The second legitimate use is the reflexive use. It comes into play in any clause in which both (1) the subject and (2) the object of either a verb or a preposition refer to the same person: *I saw myself in a new light. I need to look out for myself.*

The rules involving the emphatic (or intensive) and the reflexive uses of *myself* apply as well to the other compound personal pronouns.

 There is even a Save icon, to reassure yourself that your draft has been saved.... (*New York Times*)

The reflexive use of *yourself* is inappropriate here, because the subject of the independent clause is *icon,* not *you*.

Quick fix: substitute *you* for *yourself.*

 Mr. Eichner does a great job of controlling the physical space between him and his subjects.... (*New York Times*)

Quick fix: substitute *himself* for *him.*

33   Give this advice to whoever asks—and to whomever else it might be useful.

Some grammarians, editors, and authorities on usage are just about ready to give up on preserving the distinction between *who* and *whom* (and between *whoever* and *whomever*). A few, in fact, have already thrown in the towel. But those experts are selling the public short. In conversation, of course, we're unlikely to be taken to task for misusing such pronouns, but we can easily learn how to make the right choice when we're composing a sentence to be read. It's helpful to remember that *who* and *whoever* are subjective pronouns (and therefore see duty as the subjects of clauses) and that *whom* and *whomever* are objective pronouns (and thus play the part of objects of prepositions and objects of verbs). That knowledge alone, though, isn't always enough to ensure that we'll feel confident in choosing the appropriate pronoun. Fortunately, all we need to learn is how to manage the four kinds of constructions in which *who*, *whoever*, *whom*, and *whomever* commonly appear.

1. *Who* or *whom* (or *whoever* or *whomever*) in an independent clause

If *who* or *whom* (or *whoever* or *whomever*) is called for in an independent clause, that independent clause is almost certain to be phrased as a question. And because it's a question, the phrasing won't follow the customary word order that readers expect in a sentence. So you need to rearrange the words of the clause into standard, declarative order, and ask yourself which pronoun—*she* or *they*, or *her* or *them*—you could substitute for *who* or *whom* (or *whoever* or *whomever*). If either *she* or *they* fits, you need the subjective pronoun *who* (or *whoever*). If either *her* or *them* fits, you need the objective pronoun *whom* (or *whomever*).

If you were attacked by pirates, who would you want by your side? (*Wall Street Journal*)

You can easily reorder *who would you want by your side* into *you would want who by your side*. Putting *she* or *they* in place of *who* would produce nonsense, but *her* or *them* would work perfectly—so *whom* is correct. The grammatical explanation? *Whom* is the direct object of the verb *want*. Any pronoun serving as a direct object needs to be an objective pronoun.

2. *Who* or *whom* (or *whoever* or *whomever*) in an adjectival dependent clause

An adjectival dependent clause beginning with *who*, *whom*, *whoever*, or *whomever* is a dependent clause that describes a person. The simple way to determine which pronoun is correct is to sequester the adjectival dependent clause from the rest of the sentence. After you've isolated the dependent clause, rephrase its contents into standard word order. Then ask yourself whether a subjective pronoun like *he* or *they*, or an objective pronoun like *him* or *them*, could step into *who*'s or *whom*'s (or *whoever*'s or *whomever*'s) shoes. If *he* or *they* fits, you need *who* or *whoever*; if *him* or *them* fits, you need *whom* or *whomever*.

She said she first contacted the congressman, who she called "the wonderful Anthony Weiner," over Facebook in mid-August.... (*New York Times*)

Segregate the adjectival dependent clause *who she called "the wonderful Anthony Weiner,"* then rephrase it as *she called who "the wonderful Anthony Weiner"*—and there's no way you would not substitute *him* for *who*. The clause thus needs the objective pronoun *whom*, which serves as the direct object of *called*.

3. *Who* or *whom* (or *whoever* or *whomever*) in a nominative dependent clause

A nominative dependent clause is a dependent clause that functions like a single-word noun, and thus it can serve as the object of a preposition or as the object of a verb. To decide whether *who* or *whom* (or *whoever* or *whomever*) is the correct pronoun for a nominative dependent clause, you can follow the same steps you followed with adjectival dependent clauses.

 If "Beautiful Thing" were to be made into a film, Shetty would be played by whomever is the current Bollywood equivalent of Paul Giamatti. (*New York Times*)

Some readers will argue that *whomever* is the correct pronoun for that sentence. They will claim that *whomever* is the object of the preposition *by*—and therefore *whoever* would be wrong. But their argument quickly falls apart. The object of the preposition *by* is in fact the entire nominative dependent clause *whomever is the current Bollywood equivalent of Paul Giamatti*. Now which pronoun could you substitute for *whomever* in that clause? Obviously not *him*. Only *he* will do; it's a subjective pronoun serving as the subject of the clause.

Quick fix: substitute *whoever* for *whomever*.

4. *Who* or *whom* (or *whoever* or *whomever*) in an adjectival dependent clause in which another clause is embedded

More complicated than the sentences we've examined thus far are sentences in which an adjectival dependent clause includes within it yet another clause—a very short clause consisting of only a subject and a verb of saying (such as *stated* or *declared*) or of thinking (such as *considered* or *decided*). When you're trying to decide whether *who* or *whom* (or *whoever* or *whomever*) is the right choice for a sentence like that, force yourself to ignore the clause-within-a-clause. That clause, which has no influence at all on whether you need *who* or *whom* (or *whoever* or *whomever*), can easily distract you. Mentally—or even physically—cross out the clause-within-a-clause, and treat the adjectival dependent clause as you would treat any of the others that were discussed above.

 Staley asked Diederich about rum punch, which prompted a long story about "the old guy César" at the Grand Hotel Oloffson, in Port-au-Prince, whom Greene thought made the best one. (*New Yorker*)

The complete adjectival dependent clause is *whom Greene thought made the best one*, and the clause-within-a-clause is *Greene thought*. Mentally subtract the clause-within-a-clause, and you're left with *whom made the best one*. The pronoun *whom* is obviously wrong; you could not replace it with an objective pronoun such as *him*.

Quick fix: substitute *who* for *whom*.

There's another way to look at an adjectival dependent clause that includes another clause within it. Instead of mentally crossing out the clause-within-a-clause, you can retain it—and then mentally rephrase the entire construction in standard word order. In the erroneous example immediately above, for instance, the words forming the construction *whom Greene thought made the best one* can be resequenced as *Greene thought whom made the best one*. Only a subjective pronoun can follow *thought*; nobody would write *Greene thought him made the best one*.

34 This is in reference to your pronoun without a clear antecedent.

Think of a pronoun as the shadow of a noun. When the light is just right and a sentence is not crowded with nouns, a reader has no trouble making out which noun in a sentence is casting any one particular shadow. But the light is often less than ideal, and sentences all too often are heavily furnished with nouns. It's no wonder, then, that readers get frustrated when they can't track a shadow back to its source. Grammarians call that source an antecedent—a word literally meaning *that which comes before*. Sentences in which the antecedent of a pronoun is not instantly evident suffer from what are commonly called errors in pronoun reference.

This chapter covers eight ways to avoid pronoun-reference errors. (The pronoun *it* merits a chapter all to itself.)

1. Don't let multiple nouns compete for antecedental status.

 I tell people to immediately report vexatious neighbors to the police so that when they finally shoot their dog or key their Hummer, an extensive paper trail will document the neighbor's previous transgressions. They never call the cops. (*Wall Street Journal*) [Note, too, the erroneous shift from the plural *neighbors* to the singular-possessive *neighbor's*.]

Competing for status as the antecedent of the pronouns *they* and *their* are three nouns: *people* (the subject of an infinitive), *neighbors* (the direct object of an infinitive), and *police* (the object of a preposition). The first time a reader makes her way through the sentence, she can be forgiven for mistakenly thinking that the victims have turned vengeful and that they're the ones who shot the vexatious neighbors' dog or keyed the neighbors' Hummer.

 I tell people to immediately report a vexatious neighbor to the police department so that when he finally shoots their dog or keys their Hummer, an extensive paper trail will document his previous transgressions. They never call the cops. [Troubled by the split infinitive **to** *immediately report*? See Chapter 52.]

2. Subjects make strong antecedents; objects of prepositions make flimsier antecedents.

 While general-admission tickets to the shows aren't available, websites will live-stream many of them. (*Wall Street Journal*)

The noun *tickets* has a stronger claim than *shows* to being the antecedent of *them*, because *tickets* is the subject of a clause and *shows* is just the humble object of a preposition. So a reader might have to do a double take before figuring out that *shows* is the intended antecedent.

Web sites will live-stream many of the shows for which general-admission tickets aren't available.

That revision leads us to the third principle.

3. Wash that pronoun right out of the sentence.

A troublesome pronoun sometimes lacks any good reason to be hanging around in a sentence in the first place. With a bit of rephrasing, such a pronoun can be quietly subtracted from the sentence.

A poster is worth a thousand words. That's the gist of "Drew: The Man Behind the Poster," a documentary valentine to Drew Struzan, a semiretired top-tier illustrator whose promotional designs for countless movies—among them the "Indiana Jones," "Star Wars" and Muppet franchises—have greatly defined their image in the collective consciousness. (*New York Times*)

The pronoun *their,* toward the end of the second sentence, is tugged more forcefully toward *designs* (the subject of an adjectival dependent clause) than toward *movies* (the mere object of a preposition) or toward the list of movie franchises fenced off behind dashes. The sentence can easily be refashioned, though, to dispose of the pronoun.

That's the gist of "Drew: The Man Behind the Poster," a documentary valentine to Drew Struzan, a semiretired top-tier illustrator whose promotional designs have greatly defined the images of countless movies—among them the "Indiana Jones," "Star Wars," and Muppet franchises—in the collective consciousness.

4. Don't fall for far-flung antecedents.

A pronoun needs to be within reach of its antecedent. Pronouns and their antecedents cannot survive long-distance relationships.

Noise-canceling (NC) headphones don't actually reduce irregular noises like speech and crying babies in the row behind you. Even so, cutting down airplane roar is supposed to cut down on "noise fatigue," an edgy tiredness that comes from hours-long exposure to loud noise. They also let you listen to music or videos on the train or plane at a much lower (and safer) volume. (*New York Times*)

An entire intermediary sentence separates the pronoun *they* in the third sentence from its antecedent (*headphones*) in the first sentence.

[third sentence] The headphones also let you listen to music or videos. . . .

5. An unaccompanied *this* or *that* can spell trouble.

If the antecedent of *this* or *that* is not instantly clear, you often need to do no more than insert a clarifiant noun after the pronoun. The bracketed, boldfaced noun in the second of the following two sentences would spare readers any confusion: *He finally learned to use spreadsheets. That [**progress**] impressed her.*

Sometimes, though, a *this* or a *that* can be unusually mischievous.

At its height, Sears was the country's biggest retailer. But that has not been true for more than two decades and now, the department store chain, struggling to execute on its latest turnaround, is looking to shrink again. (*New York Times*)

What is a reader to make of the pronoun *that* at the head of the second sentence? Exactly what is it that hasn't been true for more than two decades? Is the reader to infer that with the passage of more than twenty years, the truthfulness of what the first sentence is declaring has been nullified—in other words, that never, even at its height, was Sears the country's biggest retailer? Only after a few seconds of reflection is a reader likely to unpuzzle what the writer meant.

Until two decades or so ago, Sears was the country's biggest retailer. But now the department-store chain, struggling to execute on its latest turnaround, is looking to shrink again.

6. Flee from wicked *whiches*.

A reader has every right to expect that the pronoun *which* will be immediately preceded by an explicit antecedent, as in *She sold me her Honda Civic, which she had bought in 2011.* But writers often renege on their obligations.

Solid-state drives are also quieter than hard drives and don't consume as much power, which extends battery life. Solid-state drives also generate less heat, which can make computers run cooler. (*New York Times*)

The reader of that two-sentence excerpt is hagridden by two *which*es. In the first sentence, *power* obviously cannot serve as the antecedent of *which*. The pronoun lacks any clear-cut antecedent in the sentential surround, and the sentence, in fact, can make do without the pronoun at all.

Solid-state drives are also quieter than hard drives and don't consume as much power, thereby extending battery life.

The *which* in the second sentence also lacks an explicit antecedent and can also be revised right out of the phrasing.

Solid-state drives also generate less heat and thus can make computers run cooler.

7. An adjective can never an antecedent be.

The antecedent of a pronoun must be a noun (or another pronoun, or a phrase or a dependent clause functioning as a noun). A word serving as an adjective can never function as an antecedent.

 Fany Gerson, who started her paleta business, La Newyorkina, out of a cart at the Hester Street Fair some four years ago, now sells them to markets all over town.... (*New York Times*)

The pronoun-reference error (the noun *paleta* is comporting itself adjectivally, modifying the noun *business*, and therefore cannot serve as the antecedent of *them*) is compounded by an error in pronoun-antecedent agreement (see Chapter 29), because the pronoun *them* is plural.

 Fany Gerson, who started her business, La Newyorkina, by selling paletas out of a cart at the Hester Street Fair some four years ago, now sells them to markets all over town.... OR: Fany Gerson, who started her paleta business ... four years ago, now sells the paletas to markets all over town.... OR: ... now sells the Mexican ice pops to markets all over town....

8. Don't let a possessive noun impersonate an antecedent.

Grammarians insist that a nonpossessive pronoun (such as *she*) cannot have a possessive noun (such as *Melinda's*) as its antecedent.

 Melinda's latest paintings demonstrate that she has mastered abstraction.

A noun in possessive form, after all, functions as an adjective—and, again, only a noun (or a noun-equivalent) can serve as the antecedent of a pronoun.

 Relatives of Stephen Schneider's patients asked him about all the opioids they were taking. (photo caption, *New Yorker*)

 Relatives of patients treated by Stephen Schneider asked him about all the opioids he was prescribing.

A possessive pronoun, of course, can have a possessive noun as its antecedent: *Melinda's latest paintings demonstrate her mastery of abstraction.*

35 The Itty-Bitty Pronoun That Causes Great Big Trouble

If we're not careful, the tiny pronoun *it* can turn into a two-letter terror and make our readers' lives miserable. *It*, like most other pronouns, is used correctly only when it has an antecedent—a noun (or, in some cases, another pronoun) to which it unmistakably refers. If our readers can't instantly trace the pronoun back to its antecedent, we've wasted their time.

The first problem to avoid is using *it* without an explicit antecedent, as in the following sentence, about entering a crowded restaurant.

 You know you will be bumped and jostled, but you don't know which direction it will come from. (*New York Times*)

The pronoun *it* lacks a nounal antecedent. The writer might well have had *bumping* and *jostling* (gerunds, or verbal forms that function as nouns) in mind as the antecedents of *it*, but *bumped* and *jostled*, the words that materialized in the sentence, are past participles (verbal forms that function as adjectives) and therefore can't serve as antecedents. (A further problem, of course, is that the phantom antecedent is plural, and thus there's an error in pronoun-antecedent agreement as well [see Chapter 29].) An easy way out is to rephrase the sentence by disposing of *it*.

You know you will be bumped and jostled, but you don't know from which direction.

A second problem arises when the antecedent of *it* is in possessive form. A noun in possessive form cannot serve as the antecedent of *it* (or of any other pronoun [see Chapter 34])—because such a noun is functioning adjectivally. Only a possessive pronoun can have a possessive noun or a possessive pronoun as its antecedent.

Google's disappointing results were particularly surprising because it rarely misses analysts' expectations.... (*New York Times*)

Google's can't serve as the antecedent of the nonpossessive pronoun *it*.

Google's disappointing results were particularly surprising, because the company rarely misses analysts' expectations....

A third (and far more exasperating) problem occurs when the pronoun *it* appears more than once, each time with a different antecedent, as in the third sentence of the excerpt below.

After spending more than $5 million on the research, Nascar spent millions more buying back its digital rights in 2013 from Turner, which had paid Nascar a fee to run its Web site. This will help resolve conflicts that have hampered Nascar's exposure. For instance, a television station currently can shoot video at a track and broadcast it, but it has not been allowed to post the video on its Web site because it competes with Turner's Web site. (*New York Times*)

In the last sentence of the excerpt, *it* appears three times, and *its* appears once. The first *it* has *video* as its antecedent; the second *it* and the possessive pronoun *its* have *television station* as their antecedent; and the third *it* has *Web site* as its antecedent. But readers shouldn't be burdened with having to sort things out for themselves.

For instance, a television station can currently shoot and broadcast video from a track, but it hasn't been allowed to post the video online, because its Web site is in competition with Turner's.

In the revision, we're down to only two pronouns, each with *television station* as its antecedent. Readers are unlikely to be confused.

The fourth problem to avoid is writing a sentence (or two consecutive sentences) in which the pronoun *it* appears in the immediate vicinity of the expletive *it*. In fact, few sentences are big enough for both the pronoun and the expletive. The expletive *it* is a word without any meaning at all: it's merely a prop, a support, pushed into place so that a word-group can hold itself up as a grammatically complete clause. The *it* in the sentence *It is snowing* has no antecedent; the word doesn't refer back to anything else. The expletive *it* isn't a pronoun—but is easily mistaken for one.

 … [the play] "Wit" gently reminds us of how the seemingly infinite mind divorces itself from the finiteness of the body that sustains it. The industry of thought gets us through life, until life abruptly makes it known that it is disposing of us. (*New York Times*) [The comma before *until* should be omitted; see Chapter 73.]

In the first sentence of the excerpt, both *itself* and *it* share *mind* as the antecedent. In the second sentence, though, the first *it* is an expletive, and the second *it* is a pronoun—but the status of each *it* won't be immediately apparent to some readers.

 The industry of thought gets us through life until life abruptly declares that it is disposing of us.

Finally, never write a sentence that forces a single *it* to function simultaneously in two different capacities—both as a pronoun with an explicit antecedent and as an expletive.

 While the textbook industry is ripe for innovation, it already is a crowded market and has been tough for changes to occur. (*Wall Street Journal*)

In the independent clause, *it* is followed by two verb phrases. The verb phrase *already is a crowded market* requires *it* to be a pronoun, whose antecedent is *textbook industry*. The second verb phrase, *has been tough for changes to occur,* requires *it* to be an expletive. But *it* can't be both things at once.

 While the textbook industry is ripe for innovation, it already is a crowded market and is inhospitable to change.

Countererrorist Measures

36 Beyond Compare—in the Worst Way

It's perfectly logical to compare (or contrast) one restaurant with another, or one chef with another—but it would be folly to compare a restaurant with a chef, or a chef with a menu. Comparisons are valid only when the two things or persons being compared are members of a single category or class. Sentences attempting to express a comparison (or a contrast) often sink sadly into the senseless. Screwball comparisons abound.

 Compared with the lower floors, the population on the upper floors is more rarefied. (*New York Times*)

Lower floors are being compared with a population.

 Compared with the lower floors, the upper floors have a more rarefied population.

 His [the chef's] voice boomed manically around the matchbox space, and in comparison with other, more classically decorous sushi joints in town, the helter-skelter choreography with his (equally large, non-Japanese) sous-chef seemed almost comically awkward. (*New York*)

A category of restaurants is being compared with the behavior of a chef and his sous-chef in one particular restaurant in that category.

 …and in comparison with the more classical decorum of other sushi joints in town, the helter-skelter choreography with his (equally large, non-Japanese) sous-chef seemed almost comically awkward.

 In February, the magazine Consumer Reports rated the chain's [McDonald's] drip coffee as better-tasting than Starbucks. (*Wall Street Journal*)

McDonald's drip coffee (a beverage) is being compared with Starbucks (a chain of coffeehouses).

 In February, the magazine Consumer Reports rated the chain's drip coffee as better-tasting than Starbucks's.

With the conversion of the noun *Starbucks* to the possessive form, *drip coffee* is implied after *Starbucks's*.

 Amazon's library of streaming music is tiny compared with Spotify or Pandora, but it might be fine if you have a phone full of MP3s. (*New York Times*)

One service's library of streaming music is being compared with one competing service or another.

 Amazon's library of streaming music is tiny compared with that of Spotify or Pandora....

 In the end, the women's clothes, and many of the models, were indistinguishable from previous HBA [Hood by Air] shows, which is to say that they were genderless, or gender mixed. (*New York*)

Clothes (and many models) are being compared with previous HBA shows.

 ...the women's clothes, and many of the models, were indistinguishable from those in previous HBA shows....

We've seen that in resolving a faulty comparison we can avoid the awkward repetition of a noun by using phrasing such as *that of* or *those of*. Sometimes, though, a writer takes things too far and ends up with what might be called a surplus-possessive construction.

 He found Mr. [Kim] Cesarion, and was captivated by... his falsetto, similar to that of Michael Jackson's. (*Wall Street Journal*)

The phrasing *that of* is redundant, because the noun *Michael Jackson* has already been converted to possessive form with an apostrophe and an *s*.

 ...his falsetto, similar to Michael Jackson's. OR:... his falsetto, similar to that of Michael Jackson.

37 Falling In and Out of Like

You might not want to start a sentence with the preposition *like* unless you know in your bones that you're a person with a strong sense of direction and follow-through in your thinking and writing. That simple little preposition, after all, is going to acquire a noun (or sometimes a pronoun) as its object; and as soon as your reader takes in the full sweep of your introductory prepositional phrase, she'll expect it to be followed by one thing and one thing only: an independent clause whose subject is a noun (or a pronoun) that belongs to the very same class of persons or things as the object of the preposition at the outset of your sentence. Any other sort of subject will plunge the sentence into illogic.

 Like Mr. Bush, his [Mike Huckabee's] approach to politics seems... highly emotional.... (*Wall Street Journal*)

A former president is being likened to an approach.

 Like Mr. Bush, Mr. Huckabee seems to approach politics in a highly emotional way....

A writer can get things right in the first sentence of a sequence, then bollix things up in the second.

 Like Otto, Rudi was a Czech. Like Otto, his birthplace varies from record to record. (*The Girls: Sappho Goes to Hollywood* [St. Martin's Press], by Diane McLellan)

In the first sentence, one man is likened to another. So far, so good. But in the second sentence, a man is being likened to a birthplace.

 Like Otto's, his birthplace varies from record to record. [The noun *birthplace* is implied after *Otto's*.] OR: Like Otto's birthplace, Rudi's varies from record to record.

 Like [Bob] Hope, he [Bugs Bunny] was usually paired with a more inward character who loves to sing (Daffy Duck is Bugs's Bing [Crosby], though blustery rather than cool), and, like Hope, his appeal rises entirely from the limitless brashness and self-confidence with which he approaches even the most threatening circumstances. (*New Yorker*)

In the third independent clause of the sentence, Bob Hope is being likened to the appeal of a cartoon character.

 … like Hope's, his appeal rises entirely from the limitless brashness. …

The quickest fix sometimes involves ditching the preposition *like* and substituting *as in* or *as with*.

 And like any good marriage, everyone gets something out of the deal. (*New York*)

A good marriage is being likened to everyone.

 And as in any good marriage, everyone gets something out of the deal.

Many writers have as much trouble with the preposition *unlike* as they do with *like*.

 Unlike painkillers such as aspirin or Tylenol, consuming large quantities [of opioids] is unlikely to permanently damage the organs. (*New Yorker*) [Is the split infinitive in this sentence an avoidable distraction? See Chapter 52.]

Painkillers are being contrasted with consuming.

 Opioids, unlike painkillers such as aspirin and Tylenol, are unlikely to damage organs permanently when consumed in large quantities. OR: Unlike painkillers such as aspirin and Tylenol, opioids are unlikely to cause permanent organ damage when consumed in large quantities. [Some readers, though, might object to the appearance of both *unlike* and *unlikely* in such a short sentence. A further revision: In contrast to painkillers such as aspirin and Tylenol, opioids are unlikely to cause permanent organ damage when consumed in large quantities.]

38 Comparatives are odious when superlatives are better.

Adjectives have their work cut out for them. Not only do they have to be on call in their standard forms (such as *pink* and *comfortable*), which a grammarian would call their positive forms. But they also need to be ready at a moment's notice for duty in what are known as their comparative and superlative forms.

You reach for the comparative form of an adjective when you're comparing two persons or things: *She's the younger of the sisters. She's more intelligent than her brother.* You need the superlative form of an adjective when you want your readers to understand that one of three or more persons or things has the highest or lowest degree of a particular quality: *She's the wittiest of the sisters. She's the most intelligent of the interns.*

You can produce the comparative form in two ways. When the adjective is only one or two syllables long, all you need to do is tack on an *er* (or, if the adjective—like *strange*—already ends in *e*, just an *r*). For a longer adjective, insert the adverb *more* or *less* in front of it.

You can also produce the superlative form in two ways. For a short adjective, add *est* (if the adjective ends in *e*, add *st* only). For a longer adjective, slip the adverb *most* or *least* directly in front.

Things get complicated when two or more comparative or superlative forms are arranged in a row. Take care to position adjectives ending in *er* or *est* before adjectival phrases that begin with *more, most, less,* or *least.*

 After all, paying someone ten million dollars isn't going to make that person more creative or smarter. (*New Yorker*)

A reader can't help mentally pushing the adverb *more* forward in the sentence so that it lands in front of *smarter*. The unhappy result? The person is more smarter.

 … paying someone ten million dollars isn't going to make that person smarter or more creative.

 The activity also makes clear a fact that most scientists keep trying to underscore, that the best, most exciting and cheapest science involves unmanned spacecraft. (*New York Times*)

 …the best, most exciting, and least expensive science involves unmanned spacecraft.

Now have a look again at the title of this chapter. Why doesn't it say "superlatives are best"? *Best*, after all, is the superlative form of the adjective *good*. (The comparative form is *better*.) In the title, though, only two things are being compared—the comparative form and the superlative form. When you're comparing just two things, you need a comparative adjective, not a superlative. You would never want to say of one half of a pair of twins that *Anna is the brightest*; you would say *Anna is the brighter*.

 What's Best, LED or Incandescent Lights? (headline, *New York Times*)

Which Are Better, LED or Incandescent Lights?

39 This chapter is not as good or better than the others.

There's a gaping hole in the title of this chapter.
   Hint: a word is missing.
   Haven't found it yet?
   Then let's break the title down into two fun-size chunkettes and see what it's really saying:
   1. This chapter is not as good the others.
   2. This chapter is not better than the others.

The second statement obviously makes sense. But the first? The error laying waste to it is called an incomplete comparison.

All too often, an editorial search party needs to be organized to bring the second *as* in an *as+adjective+as* phrase back to civilization.

 This FX series, which starts on Wednesday, should be as good or better than the original. (*New York Times*)

 This FX series ... should be as good as or better than the original.

 An April report by the Center for American Progress looked at U.S. women who earn as much or more than their husbands.... (*Wall Street Journal*)

 An April report ... looked at U.S. women who earn as much as or more than their husbands....

As, however, isn't the only word that can wander off from a comparison.

 Yet New Orleans's overall rate of violent crime is on par or lower than that of other cities its size. (*Wall Street Journal*)

 Yet New Orleans's overall rate of violent crime is on par with or lower than that of other cities its size.

40 Don't leave out the *other*—or *else*.

Notice anything not quite right about the following sentence, which gamely attempts to express a contrast?

 Rachel Kushner's second novel, "The Flamethrowers," unfolds on a bigger, brighter screen than nearly any recent American novel I can remember. (*New York Times*) [Note: the review from which the sentence is excerpted appeared in the very same month that the novel under consideration was published.]

Give up? Then consider this: you would never declare that *Burger King is better than any fast-food restaurant.* And why not? Because by doing so, you would unintentionally be ousting Burger King from the very class of things to which it belongs—namely, fast-food restaurants. But the writer of the first excerpt above is doing much the same thing: he's saying, in effect, that *The Flamethrowers* is not "any recent American novel [he] can remember." What's missing from his sentence, as well as from the sentence about Burger King, is the adjective *other: Burger King is better than any other fast food-restaurant.* (Burger King has now been restored to the category to which it belongs.)

 Rachel Kushner's second novel ... unfolds on a bigger, brighter screen than nearly any other recent American novel I can remember.

The adjective *other* isn't the only word that goes missing from a lot of sentences, to the detriment of the meaning and the logic. See if you can find what's amiss in the sentence below.

 From her first televised "y'all" in 1999, Paula Deen has worked harder to promote Southern food than anyone in the modern media era, wielding frosted hair and frosted doughnuts as her weapons. (*New York Times*)

The sentence would have us believe that Deen is *not* "anyone in the modern media era." The purpose of the sentence, though, was to contrast Deen with others in that very same era.

 ... Paula Deen has worked harder to promote Southern food than anyone else in the modern media era. ...

Sometimes a single sentence suffers from two varieties of incomplete comparison.

 ... he's singing Porter and Razaf as well or better than anyone. (*Village Voice*)

 ... he's singing Porter and Razaf as well as or better than anyone else.

41 One of these things is not like the others.

The business of writing sentences often calls for you to present three or more items in a series (*a, b, and c*). The ideal series—the sort that will please prickly readers and exacting grammarians alike—is one in which all of the items belong to a single grammatical family. They could all be nouns, for instance, or they could all be prepositional phrases, or they could all be adverbial dependent clauses. Think of the items in the series as grammatical siblings: they need to share a single, immediately identifiable, vivid grammatical feature. They must be identical in their genes.

When the family resemblance is recognizable, the series is said to be parallel. Parallelism is nothing more than the comforting similarity in grammatical form of the items arranged in a list. If the first item in the list is an adjective, then the other items must also be adjectival in behavior. They could be single-word adjectives, or adjectival phrases (such as prepositional phrases serving as adjectives), or any other sorts of word-groups that are adjectival in their conduct. As long as each of the items in the mix is an adjective or a phrasal or clausal equivalent of an adjective, the parallelism will be flawless.

The parallelism in sentences easily goes kablooey, though, and it does so in predictable ways. Have a look at a three-sentence paragraph.

> It didn't hurt that [Stefan] Zweig had been born very wealthy, knew everyone and did whatever he pleased, lived however and wherever he wished. He was exceptionally well read, fluent in many languages and had the rare gift of endearing himself to individuals of all walks, from world-famous figures like Freud, Joyce, Einstein, Toscanini and Rodin down to the regulars of cafés in Vienna, Berlin and Paris. He recognized his luck, knew he had been spared the debilitating hardships of hackdom, and throughout his life he remained unstintingly generous to writers and artists in need of help. (*Wall Street Journal*)

The parallelism in the first sentence is impeccable. The series in the sentence consists of three verb phrases, which can be arrayed vertically as follows:

(A) had been born very wealthy
(B) knew everyone and did whatever he pleased
   and
(C) lived however and wherever he wished

You can easily double-check the status of the parallelism by asking yourself whether the insertion of the noun *Zweig* or the pronoun *He* at the start of each phrase would generate a grammatically complete sentence. The answer for each phrase would be yes.

Things start to fall apart, however, in the second sentence, which includes three series. Below are the elements in the first of the three series:

(A) was exceptionally well read
(B) fluent in many languages
   and
(C) had the rare gift of endearing himself to individuals of all walks

A and C are parallel verb phrases; you could insert *Zweig* or *He* at the start of each to form a complete sentence. B, however, is an adjectival phrase and could not be expanded into a complete sentence if you added *Zweig* or *He* at the beginning. You would need to add the verb *was* before *fluent*. The easiest way to achieve parallelism in the series, then, is to expand the B element into a verb phrase:

  (B) was fluent in many languages

(The second series in the sentence [*Freud, Joyce, Einstein, Toscanini, and Rodin*] and the third series [*Vienna, Berlin, and Paris*] are perfectly parallel: the elements in each of those series are nouns.)

The third and final sentence in the paragraph also includes a nonparallel series, although there are two ways of looking at the problem. A first list of the elements in the series looks like this:

(A) recognized his luck
(B) knew he had been spared the debilitating hardships of hackdom
and
(C) throughout his life he remained unstintingly generous to writers and artists in need of help

A and B are parallel verb phrases (they could be expanded into complete sentences by positioning *Zweig* or *He* at the beginning), but C is an independent clause (it's already the equivalent of a complete sentence). Deleting *he* from the final element will result in a list of parallel verb phrases.

There's a second way, though, of looking at that final series:

(A) He recognized his luck
(B) knew he had been spared the debilitating hardships of hackdom
and
(C) throughout his life he remained unstintingly generous to writers and artists in need of help

When you look at the series this way, you recognize that A and C are parallel independent clauses and that B, as a verb phrase, is the nonparallel element. The faulty parallelism, then, can be resolved by inserting the pronoun *he* at the start of B. The series will now consist of three parallel independent clauses.

The most common variety of faulty parallelism, in sum, is the sort in which one item in a list fails to match the other items in grammatical form. Flubbed parallelism can often be resolved in more than one way.

 A couple of hours later, his American Express card was used at a liquor store, a drugstore, and at a Chinese restaurant in a strip mall about thirty miles away. (*New Yorker*)

 …his American Express card was used at a liquor store, at a drugstore, and at a Chinese restaurant.... [three parallel prepositional phrases] OR:… his American Express card was used at a liquor store, a drugstore, and a Chinese restaurant.... [three parallel nounal elements functioning as the objects of the preposition *at*]

A second kind of faulty parallelism results from the writer's inconsistent use of what grammarians call determiners—the articles *a, an,* and *the,* as well as possessive pronouns (such as *her* and *their*) and nouns in possessive form (such as *Hannah's* and *Mother's*). If a single determiner fits with each item in the list, you can either include it before each item or insert it only once—in front of the very first item. Often, however, a single determiner will not fit with each item in the list, so a suitable determiner must be inserted before each. In some lists, one item might be incompatible with an indefinite article (neither *a* nor *an* will fit) and thus needs to appear without an article preceding it.

 A typical off-duty outfit involves a black blazer, white T-shirt, jeans, and a scarf. (*Harper's Bazaar*)

(A) a black blazer [determiner followed by a noun phrase]
(B) white T-shirt [noun phrase compatible with the article *a*]
(C) jeans [a noun incompatible with the article *a*]
   and
(D) a scarf [determiner followed by a noun]

 (B) a white T-shirt [determiner followed by noun]

The article *an* precedes words beginning with a vowel sound, and *a* precedes words beginning with a consonant sound.

 ... Leigh Hunt was a poet, editor, and essayist.... (*New Yorker*)

 ... Leigh Hunt was a poet, an editor, and an essayist....

A third category of faulty parallelism afflicts sentences in which a helping verb (also known as an auxiliary verb) has not been included when it is needed in front of each main verb. If a single helping verb fits with all of the main verbs in a series, the helping verb can be inserted before each main verb, or it can be inserted only once—in front of the very first main verb in the series. Sometimes, however, a single helping verb will not mesh with one or more of the main verbs in a sentence. Each main verb will therefore need its own helping verb.

 George Lewis, Jr., ... was born in the Dominican Republic, raised in Florida, and is now based in L.A. ... (*New Yorker*)

(A) was born in the Dominican Republic
(B) raised in Florida
   and
(C) is now based in L.A.

 (B) was raised in Florida OR [eliminating the need for a helping verb]: grew up in Florida

Faulty parallelism is not limited to sentences that present lists; see Chapters 42 and 43.

42 Reconcilable Differences

Never upset the domestic harmony in a sentence in which you're using a correlative conjunction. Each of the correlative conjunctions consists of words partnered into couples. The most common are *either... or; neither... nor; not only... but also* (a variation is *not just... but also*); and *both... and*. (The *also* in *not only... but also* and in *not just... but also* is sometimes omitted, with no harm done.)

The grammatical system of a sentence that includes a correlative conjunction achieves equilibrium when the phrasing that follows the first half of the correlative-conjunction pair (*either, neither, not only,* or *both*) perfectly balances the phrasing that follows the second half of the pair (*or, nor, but also,* or *and*).

What comes after the first half, in other words, must be the grammatical soul mate of what comes after the second half—or else there will be no peace in your sentence.

Can you find the source of the discord in each of the following excerpts?

 ... his engineering skills weren't equal to either the quality of his own instrument or to Bear's precise, fluid drumming. (*New Yorker*)

 ... "4 Months, 3 Weeks and 2 Days" flinches neither from the procedures nor the outcome of his trade. (*New Yorker*)

 ... Harold Ross... was apparently not only aware of Mitchell's composites but encouraged him. (*New Yorker*)

 ... one of Ms. Lockwood's great gifts as a poet is her ability both to subvert and revel in porn's stock language and images. (*New York Times*)

If the errors weren't instantly apparent to you, take a second look at the sentences, now that each correlative conjunction has been boldfaced and the phrasing following each half of the correlative-conjunction couple has been underlined.

 ... his engineering skills weren't equal to **either** <u>the quality of his own instrument</u> **or** <u>to Bear's precise, fluid drumming</u>.

 ... "4 Months, 3 Weeks and 2 Days" flinches **neither** <u>from the procedures</u> **nor** <u>the outcome of his trade</u>.

 ... Harold Ross... was apparently **not only** <u>aware of Mitchell's composites</u> **but** <u>encouraged him</u>.

 ... one of Ms. Lockwood's great gifts as a poet is her ability **both** <u>to subvert</u> **and** <u>revel in porn's stock language and images</u>.

Are you starting to see the grammatical imbalances? In the first sentence, a noun phrase follows *either,* but a prepositional phrase follows *or.* In the second sentence, a prepositional phrase follows *neither,* but a noun phrase follows *nor.* In sentence three, an adjectival phrase follows *not only,* but a verb phrase follows *but.* In sentence four, an infinitive follows *both,* but a verb phrase follows *and.* Don't worry if you don't yet grasp all of the grammatical terminology that has been used to classify the categories of phrasing. All you need to understand is that in a grammatically balanced sentence, the form of the phrasing following the first half of the correlative-conjunction pair needs to be an exact grammatical match for the form of the phrasing following the second half of the pair.

Achieving the balance isn't difficult. All it takes is two little steps.

First, have a close look at the phrasing that follows the second half of the correlative-conjunction pair. What form does the phrasing take? If it's a single word, to which part of speech does it belong? Is it a noun, for instance, or an adjective? If the phrasing is a word-group, is it a prepositional phrase, for instance, or a dependent clause? The more confident you are about classifying the phrasing or at least having a feel for the contours of the phrasing, the more success you'll have in resolving the imbalance in the sentence. (Intuition is often enough to guide you.)

The first step in repairing the four erroneous sentences earlier in this chapter was already taken for you, three paragraphs above, when the phrasing following each half of the correlative-conjunction pairs was classified.

For the second step, you have two options. The first is to slide the first half of the correlative-conjunction pair backward or forward in the sentence until it comes to a rest right before the word that begins a construction that perfectly matches the grammatical form of the construction that follows the second half of the correlative-conjunction pair. And then you're done—at least in most cases. (A sentence occasionally requires some further reconstruction.) The other option is to leave the phrasing following the first half of the correlative-conjunction pair exactly as you found it and then rewrite the phrasing following the second half of the pair so that it's grammatically equivalent to the phrasing you've left untouched.

Below are repaired versions of the excerpts you looked at earlier, with the balanced phrasing underlined.

… his engineering skills weren't equal **either** <u>to the quality of his own instrument</u> **or** <u>to Bear's precise, fluid drumming</u>. [balanced prepositional phrases]

… "4 Months, 3 Weeks and 2 Days" flinches from **neither** <u>the procedures</u> **nor** <u>the outcome of his trade</u>. [balanced noun phrases]

… apparently Harold Ross … **not only** <u>was aware of Mitchell's composites</u> **but** <u>encouraged him</u>. [balanced verb phrases]

… one of Ms. Lockwood's great gifts as a poet is her ability **both** <u>to subvert</u> **and** <u>to revel in porn's stock language and images</u>. [balanced infinitival constructions]

Along with the correlative conjunctions, there are other mated expressions whose halves need to be followed by grammatically congruent phrasing. They include *not X but Y; less X than Y; more X than Y; as much X as Y; X as much as Y; not so much X as Y; and X rather than Y*.

not X but Y [*not* is sometimes contracted]

... she wasn't performing for the white male director, but for people who looked or felt something like herself. (*New Yorker*)

... she was performing not for the white male director but for people who looked or felt something like herself.

less X than Y

... but Bender and Bakkila are less interested in winning approval than in eliciting a strong reaction.... (*New Yorker*)

... but Bender and Bakkila are interested less in winning approval than in eliciting a strong reaction....

more X than Y

... Fitzgerald was more offended by pleasure than by vice.... (*New York*)

... Fitzgerald was offended more by pleasure than by vice....

as much X as Y

... Young is ... known as much for his irreverence as his comedy. (*New Republic*)

... Young is ... known as much for his irreverence as for his comedy.

X as much as Y

... he poured his genius into his life as much as his art. (*The Gilded Gutter Life of Francis Bacon* [Pantheon], by Daniel Farson)

... he poured his genius into his life as much as into his art.

not so much X as Y

What I wanted to suggest is not so much the negative aspect of these essays, which will be pretty obvious to anyone who can read, but rather my own metaphor for the process which came to dominate my thinking as I shaped this book. (*Hatchet Jobs: Writings on Contemporary Fiction* [The New Press], by Dale Peck)

What I wanted to suggest is not so much the negative aspect of these essays ... as my own metaphor for the process which came to dominate my thinking....

X rather than Y

Salinger is known to have made only one public statement on this issue and even that statement is diluted by the fact that it was in anticipation of events rather than a reaction to them. (*J. D. Salinger: A Life* [Random House], by Kenneth Slawenski)

... it was in anticipation of events rather than in reaction to them.

43 Welded Helping Verbs

Contractions can get us into trouble. Certain fussbudgets are opposed to all of them on principle (no good writer ever is, though), and some contractions (among them are the grotesqueries *she'd* and *there've*) belong in only the most informal prose. But one sort of contraction must be avoided at all costs.

He's done away with the scenario—sacrificial virgins aren't his thing—and instead features pure, full-bodied movement with hints of bacchanalian revelry. (*New Yorker*)

What, you may ask, is amiss with the contraction *He's*? If you object to it because it could mean either *He is* or the intended *He has*, you would have supporters aplenty. Even if you are perfectly fine with the undesirable ambiguity, though, the contraction would be grammatically correct only if the sentence ended with *thing*. But the sentence-spanning independent clause—into which another, dashed-off independent clause has been sandwiched—has a two-part compound predicate, the second half of which begins with *features*. The trouble is that *features* has no freestanding subject to which it might attach itself. The auxiliary verb *has* is welded to the pronoun *He* in the contraction at the start of the sentence. No matter how hard you might try, you won't succeed in prying that apostrophe and *s* loose from *He*. The contracted verb has the subject all to itself and is not about to give it up. The sentence, as phrased, is thus asking us to accept as grammatically sound the construction *He's instead features pure, full-bodied movement with hints of bacchanalian revelry*. The solution is to decontract the contraction and begin the sentence with *He has done away with the scenario....*

Worse, a writer sometimes tries to get away with forcing a welded auxiliary verb to serve as the contracted form of two entirely different verbs.

Despite its whimsical design, it's very useful and taught me a trick or two. (*New York Times*)

The reader is expected to round out *it's* to *it is* for the first half of the compound predicate and to *it has* for the second half.

Despite its whimsical design, it is very useful and has taught me a trick or two.

44 We don't want him singing, but we love his drumming.

Give the once-over to that title again. Notice something? One of the two words ending in *ing* is preceded by *him*, the other by *his*. Why two different forms of the pronoun?

The answer has everything to do with the difference between present participles and gerunds. A present participle and a gerund are both formed from a verb, and they both look exactly alike: they both have *ing* for a tail. But they don't carry themselves the same way in the rush and stir of a sentence. Try as it might, a present participle can never stop acting a little like a verb, but a gerund has had quite enough of being a verb. It wants to see what life will be like if it tries to pass itself off as a noun. And it turns out that living as a noun suits the gerund just fine.

Compare *Sheila can't stand Jody cooking* with *Sheila can't stand Jody's cooking*.

Drop the last word from the first sentence, and you'll still get the picture: Sheila is none too crazy about the guy. She has some reservations about him as a person. Add the final word again, and you get the big idea: of all the people who could be presiding over the stove, why does it have to be Jody?

But you can't lop off the last word from the second sentence without ending up with nonsense. In that sentence, Sheila doesn't have a beef with the guy himself; her beef is with his beef—and with anything else that emerges from his pots and pans. But it's only his culinary incompetence that she can't stand about him. In the second sentence, *cooking* is a gerund—a verbal noun. You could trade in the gerund for a regular old noun (like *lasagna*) or even a compound noun (like *stir-fry*), and the sentence would still be tickety-boo. Try pulling something like that on the first sentence, though, and you end up with craziness like *She can't stand Jody cassoulet*. The word that comes after *Jody* in the first sentence above still has something of the verb about it, and it's never going to change. It's a participle.

The rule, then? Any noun or pronoun preceding a gerund must be in possessive form.

But the rule is widely violated.

 The curator, Chris Sharp, privileges analog, often futile gestures, including Josh Smith painting his own name over and over (at Gitlen).... (*New Yorker*)

Josh Smith, a human being, is not a gesture; his painting his own name over and over is a gesture. The noun *Smith* thus needs to be in possessive form.

 The curator, Chris Sharp, privileges analog, often futile gestures, including Josh Smith's painting his own name over and over....

 Mr. Pincus ... came under scrutiny for his role in asking some early employees to renegotiate their stock compensation packages. Some saw the move as undermining Silicon Valley's long-held tradition of young entrepreneurs signing up at start-ups for low salaries but with the hope of an eventual payoff from big equity packages. (*Wall Street Journal*) [The first sentence needs a hyphen between *stock* and *compensation*; see Chapter 86.]

Young entrepreneurs aren't a "long-held tradition"; what the young entrepreneurs *did*—namely, their "signing up at start-ups for low salaries but with the hope of an eventual payoff from big equity packages"—is the tradition.

 ... Silicon Valley's long-held tradition of young entrepreneurs' signing up at start-ups for low salaries. ...

 The stories and essays I wrote in college were terrible, and the idea of them being published makes me physically ill. (*New Republic*)

 ... the idea of their being published makes me physically ill.

 The elevator was still on the ground floor for the longest time without us noticing. (*Rolling Stone*)

Quick fix: ... without our noticing.

A sentence with an error of the sort discussed in this chapter can usually be rephrased to avoid having to add an apostrophe and an *s* to form a possessive noun.

 There is no record of *Going Up* ever having been produced. (*A Ship Without a Sail: The Life of Lorenz Hart* [Simon & Schuster], by Gary Marmorstein)

Instead of converting the title *Going Up* to the possessive form, you could write:

 There is no record that *Going Up* has ever been produced.

Failing to convert a noun preceding a gerund to possessive form occasionally results in a sentence that appears to suffer from an error in subject-verb agreement. In the following sentence, *firms*, rather than *charging*, might at first seem to be the subject of *is*. (In its present, ungrammatical form, the sentence, with its assertion that *firms... is not always a good idea*, suffers from faulty predication [see Chapter 45] as well, not to mention a misplaced modifier [see Chapter 22].)

 The point of this section is that firms charging for everything they sell, at least directly, is not always a good idea. (*Why Popcorn Costs So Much at the Movies, and Other Pricing Puzzles* [Copernicus Books], by Richard B. McKenzie)

 ... firms' charging, at least directly, for everything they sell is not always a good idea. OR: ... it's not always a good idea for firms to charge, at least directly, for everything they sell.

45 Fault Lines

A clause is a stretch of words divided into two zones: the subject and the predicate. The subject zone has a noun or a pronoun as its most prominent feature, and that noun or pronoun can't wait to become the talk of the entire clause. Across the border in the predicate zone is a verb itching to reveal something important about the subject. In a structurally sound clause, there's a smooth verbal surface ranging all the way from the start of the subject zone to the far end of the predicate zone, and it's only by the joltless traversing of that surface that a clear statement gets itself made. But sometimes an earthquake of sorts strikes a clause, fracturing it right down the middle. The upheaval leaves the subject and the predicate on opposite sides of a fault line—and so out of alignment with each other that the two no longer make any sense together at all. The site of this rupture is the site of what grammarians call faulty predication. It will take some major reconstruction work to ensure that the subject and the predicate interconnect seamlessly.

If the timetable holds, as early as this summer the nighttime population of just 17,000, with 105,000 daytime workers, may begin to transform into a livable, walkable city, predicted to have 100,000 residents and 200,000 workers by 2050. (*New York Times*)

The subject-predicate misalignment is *the nighttime population… may begin to transform into a livable, walkable city.*

If the timetable holds, as early as this summer the suburb, with 105,000 daytime workers but a nighttime population of just 17,000, may begin to transform into a livable, walkable city. …

A laundry list of other threats—fungal diseases like root rot, a rare type of caterpillar and an invasive Japanese insect that kills hemlocks—have all caused losses. (*New York Times*)

Not only is *laundry list . . . have all caused losses* a subject-predicate misalignment (how could a list cause losses?), but there's an error in subject-verb agreement as well.

Other threats—including fungal diseases like root rot, a rare type of caterpillar, and an invasive Japanese insect that kills hemlocks—have all caused losses.

Faulty predication is especially likely to imperil a sentence with a compound predicate. By the time the writer begins to compose the second verb phrase of the predicate, she may have forgotten the subject of the first verb phrase.

Even better for VH1: the primetime audience has ballooned by more than 50 percent over the past four years to about 621,000 viewers last year, and is now ranked as the 27th most-watched cable network. (*New York Post*)

The subject-predicate misalignment is *the prime-time audience… is now ranked as the 27th-most-watched cable network.*

… and VH1 is now ranked as the 27th-most-watched cable network.

Faulty predication often incapacitates a dependent clause.

A nearby display demonstrates that the old idea of the apatosaurus having a long neck in order to reach up to eat from the tops of trees, giraffe style, wasn't physically possible. (*New Yorker*)

The subject-predicate misalignment in the nominative dependent clause is *the old idea...wasn't physically possible*.

 A nearby display refutes the old notion that it was physically possible for the apatosaurus, even with its long neck, to reach up to eat from the tops of trees, giraffe style.

Faulty predication also wrecks sentences in which a writer resorts to the construction *X is when* or *X is where*. A sentence beginning with, say, *Anxiety is when...* or *Anxiety is where...* is getting off to an illogical as well as an ungrammatical start, because anxiety isn't an event or a place. As subordinating conjunctions, *when* and *where* signal the beginning of adverbial dependent clauses. An adverbial dependent clause can never serve as the complement of a linking verb (also known as an equational verb), such as *is*. The complement needs to function either as a noun or as an adjective.

 What makes the digital street [i.e., the online world] safe is when teens and adults collectively agree to open their eyes and pay attention, communicate and collaboratively negotiate difficult situations. (*Time*)

 Teens and adults can make the digital street safe by collectively agreeing to open their eyes and pay attention....

Similarly, the common phrasing *the reason... is because* is faulty—for two reasons. First, the subordinating conjunction *because* marks the beginning of an adverbial dependent clause, and, again, such a clause cannot serve as the complement of a linking verb. Second, the phrasing *the reason... is because* is redundant: the noun *reason* clearly announces that the *cause* of something will be specified.

 The reason that we don't, at first, notice how carefully Flaubert is selecting his details is because Flaubert is working very hard to obscure this labor from us.... (*How Fiction Works* [Farrar, Straus and Giroux], by James Wood)

 The reason we don't, at first, notice how carefully Flaubert is selecting his details is that Flaubert is working very hard.... [A nominative dependent clause (*that Flaubert is working very hard to obscure this labor from us...*), which functions as a noun and can therefore serve as a complement, has been substituted for the adverbial dependent clause.] OR: We don't, at first, notice how carefully Flaubert is selecting his details, because Flaubert is working very hard....

46 Elliptical Workouts

There's a shortcut we're free to take in some of our sentences. We can get away with not repeating a word or a phrase if we're entirely confident that attentive readers can easily restore the omitted verbal matter by mentally dragging it forward from its position earlier in the sentence (or from the final stretch of the preceding sentence).

In the sentence *The portions are generous, the prices reasonable, the servers cheerful*, there's no need for the writer to repeat the verb *are* after *prices* and after *servers*. The reader can fill in the blanks, so to speak, with no trouble.

Elliptical construction is the grammatical term for phrasing in which one or more words have intentionally been left out. An elliptical construction succeeds only if whatever has been omitted from a later segment of a sentence is present earlier (and within a reasonable distance) in exactly the same form in which it's needed later on. If the earlier word or words won't fit snugly into any of the slots they need to occupy farther along in the sentence, the elliptical construction has failed.

 The colors are effulgent, the textures fleshy, the touch urgent. (*New Yorker*)

In the sentence above, from the review of an art-gallery show, the writer expects the reader to do the grunt work of singularizing the explicit, plural verb *are* so that there's no discord in subject-verb agreement following *touch*. But why not spare the reader the labor and pluralize the third noun in the series?

 The colors are effulgent, the textures fleshy, the brushstrokes urgent.

Slipshod elliptical constructions are jarring instead of soothing. They force a reader to make mental readjustments in one or more segments of a sentence. A reader should not have to pluck words out of thin air to round out a writer's careless phrasing.

A second type of faulty elliptical construction, however, demands more of a reader or an editor than resolving inconsistencies in singularity or plurality. Have a look at a headline from *The New York Times*.

 A Fraud,
Though
Easy to Spot,
Was Not

What the writer means is that the fraud had in fact not been spotted. But the reader can't carry forward *spot* to the empty slot after *not* without doing syntactic damage to the sentence. The final line, though, could be rephrased as *Was Not Caught* or *Went Uncaught*, and the rhyme would be retained.

Some faulty elliptical constructions are brain-teasers. A reader is burdened with reworking a sentence until all of its parts interlock cleanly.

 [about one of Nero's attempts to murder his mother] But just about everything that should have gone wrong didn't. (*New Yorker*)

 But just about everything that was supposed to go wrong didn't.

 Prescription drug abusers can, and are, breaking into homes in search of them. (*New York Times*)

 Prescription-drug abusers can, and do, break into homes in search of a fix.

 Mr. Manilow was still recovering from the flu . . . , and the front of the stage was lined with boxes of tissue in case he needed them. (He didn't.) (*New York Times*)

 . . . the front of the stage was lined with boxes of tissues in case he might need them. (He didn't.)

 Doesn't science "bake bread" (not to mention make money) in a way that philosophy never has? (*The Atlantic*)

 Replace *has* with *does, can,* or *will*. OR: Hasn't science "baked bread" (not to mention made money) in a way that philosophy never has?

47 Here is one of the clumsiest, if not the clumsiest, sentence ever. No, wait: *here is one of the clumsiest, if not the clumsiest, sentences ever.*

Sentences of the kind exhibited in the title of this chapter are common—and uncommonly ugly and ungrammatical.

 It is believed to be one of the largest—if not the largest—challenge grants ever offered by an individual in the region. (*Philadelphia Inquirer*)

 . . . Orson Welles's "Citizen Kane" has been overwhelmingly selected as one of the great (if not the greatest) motion pictures of all time. . . . (*New York Times*)

 By this standard, Michael Bloomberg is easily one of the worst mayors in the country—if not the worst. (*Daily Caller*)

To return to the blunderful title of this chapter: the construction *one of the clumsiest* cannot share a noun in the same form as that required by the construction *if not the clumsiest*. The first construction can be capped only with a plural noun; the second needs a singular noun.

So how to salvage such a sentence?

You could write *Here is one of the clumsiest, if not the clumsiest, of all sentences ever.* The sentence is now grammatically sound (the prepositional phrase *of all sentences ever* correctly completes both the *one of the clumsiest* and the *if not the clumsiest* constructions), but it sounds fussy and clunky. It's wordy, too.

You could also write *Here is one of the clumsiest sentences, if not the clumsiest one, ever.* That's shorter and not quite as bumbly.

But why not trim the sentence even further? *Here is possibly the clumsiest sentence ever.*

As for the *Daily Caller* specimen cited above, it can be whittled down to *By this standard, Mayor Bloomberg might easily be the worst mayor in the country.*

48 If you have questions about conditional sentences, this book has the answers.

Oh, and if you *don't* have questions about conditional sentences, this book *doesn't* have the answers? That, unfortunately, is what the title of this chapter daftly declares.

Business correspondence sometimes includes similarly daffy statements, such as *If you have any concerns, I'll be available between 8 a.m. and 5 p.m.,* and *If you need to reach me, my office number is (555) 555-5555.* The absurdity of those sentences should be evident. I'll be around between eight and five even if you don't have any concerns, and my office telephone number isn't going to change if it turns out that you don't need to reach me.

Each of the silly assertions above is a derangement of a kind of statement that grammarians classify as a conditional sentence. A conditional sentence is a complex sentence in which a dependent clause specifies the condition that must be met for the declaration in the independent clause to ring true (that is, to deliver a factually accurate statement), as in *If you meet the deadline, you'll earn a bonus.* The dependent clause in a conditional sentence usually begins with the subordinating conjunction *if.* (That sort of dependent clause is sometimes called a contingent clause.)

Writers all too often lapse into conditional constructions when the truthfulness of what's stated in an independent clause does not in fact hinge on what's stated in a dependent clause. The result is an error we might call the cockamamie conditional.

If you are a woman, the main focus of this book is on men but you may find some of the information of interest. (*Men on Strike: Why Men Are Boycotting Marriage, Fatherhood, and the American Dream—and Why It Matters* [Encounter Books], by Helen Smith)

The contents of the book are the same no matter which sex you belong to.

The main focus of this book is on men, but even if you're a woman, you may find some of the information of interest.

49 Oh, the lengths I would go to avoid this error ...

Notice anything not quite up to snuff about the title of this chapter? If not, look at another example.

One aspect of *Life* that Ross especially hated was the great length the erstwhile family magazine would go to print cheesecake photos. (*Genius in Disguise: Harold Ross of* The New Yorker [Carroll & Graf], by Thomas Kunkel)

Now suppose we inserted an innocent little adverbial prepositional phrase such as *in those days* between *to* and *print*: One aspect of *Life* that Ross especially hated was the great length the erstwhile family magazine would go to in those days print cheesecake photos.

The sentence, of course, goes immediately to pieces—unless we insert a second *to,* following *days*: . . . the great length the erstwhile family magazine would go to in those days to print cheesecake photos.

Or suppose we left the prepositional phrase *in those days* out of the picture and simply restructured the original sentence: One aspect of *Life* that Ross especially hated was the great length to which the erstwhile family magazine would go to print cheesecake photos.

See how both of those alternative sentences require a second *to*? As it turns out, the original sentence—as well as the title of this chapter—requires a second *to* as well.

Let's analyze the sentence structurally. *One aspect of* Life *that Ross especially hated was the great length [the erstwhile family magazine would go to] print cheesecake photos.* The bracketed phrasing is an adjectival dependent clause (modifying the noun *length*) with the relative pronoun *that* implied at its start: *One aspect of* Life *that Ross especially hated was the great length [that the erstwhile family magazine would go to] print cheesecake photos.* The word *to* is functioning as a preposition within that clause. Its prepositional function becomes even more obvious if we recast the adjectival dependent clause in inverted form: *One aspect of* Life *that Ross especially hated was the great length [to which the erstwhile family magazine would go] print cheesecake photos.*

The sentence, as we've seen, is in desperate need of another *to*, but a *to* functioning in an entirely different grammatical fashion—as the sign of an infinitive in the infinitive *to print*. The word *to* cannot function simultaneously as both a preposition and the sign of an infinitive. Thus, there's no way around including *to* a second time.

One aspect of *Life* that Ross especially hated was the great length the erstwhile family magazine would go to to print cheesecake photos. OR [smoother]: One aspect of *Life* that Ross especially hated was the great length to which the erstwhile family magazine would go to print cheesecake photos.

As always, though, we reserve the right to refashion the sentence—and thereby lose a *to*.

One aspect of *Life* that Ross especially hated was the near-perverse determination of the erstwhile family magazine to print cheesecake photos.

50 Time-Shifting Participial Phrases

A new form of slovenliness is showing up in sentences that begin or end with a present-participial phrase, and it's resulting in statements that are chronologically askew. There's no trouble with a sentence like *Standing at the window, she watched two men fighting on the sidewalk*, but what about a sentence like the following?

Rising to his feet, he hobbled a bit and fell again. (*New York Times*)

Two actions that occurred consecutively are being reported as if they occurred simultaneously. The writer needs to give the poor fellow a few moments to get back up on his feet before setting him hobbling off. Why not clarify the time sequence?

After rising to his feet, he hobbled a bit and fell again.

The misreporting of temporal relations—arising from the confusion of the sequential with the concurrent—reduces a sentence to incoherence. Merely inserting *after* at the start of the next sentence will also unkink the buckled timeline.

 Offering Graver coffee and a seat, Welles settled on the edge of a bed.... (*Vanity Fair*)

 After much discussion about religious thought and philosophy Mercedes [de Acosta] departed for Egypt, returning to Hollywood in the spring of 1939. (*Loving Garbo: The Story of Greta Garbo, Cecil Beaton, and Mercedes de Acosta* [Random House], by Hugo Vickers)

The quickest fix is to replace *returning* with *then returned*. Erroneous sentences of the sort under the microscope in this chapter muddle a chronological sequence by leaving out an intermediary step. Mercedes de Acosta obviously had to arrive in Egypt before she could leave it.

 "George Bellows," a major new retrospective, opens June 10 at Washington's National Gallery of Art, traveling to New York's Metropolitan Museum of Art for a Nov. 15 opening.... (*Wall Street Journal*)

Quick fix: replace *traveling* with *and later will travel*.

51 The past tense is a tense with a past.

The simple past tense (*She hired her former best friend*) isn't always perfectly adequate for whatever we need to say about something that's over and done with. A sentence that's already set in the past tense sometimes needs to take us even further back into the past. The only way we can get there is by shifting down into a tense that expresses the past *before* the past.

Grammarians call this specialized tense the past-perfect or the pluperfect. We form it by positioning the helping or auxiliary verb *had* in front of a main verb: *She had forgotten to turn off her computer before she left the house.* In that sentence, the action in the independent clause (*She had forgotten to turn off her computer*) took place before the action in the adverbial dependent clause (*before she left the house*), so the past-perfect is required in the independent clause.

Whenever we're relating even the simplest of stories, we owe it to our readers to arrange the events and actions in our narrative at clearly identifiable points along a timeline so that the sequence is instantly understandable. Our failure to make the necessary downshifts from the simple past to the past-perfect will result in prose that is chronologically disorienting.

 They all looked stone-faced, as if he didn't say anything unusual. (*Rolling Stone*)

Quick fix: replace *didn't say* with *hadn't said*.

 He went house hunting in Greenwich, Connecticut. At the time, he was the creative director of Nine West, which he cofounded six years earlier. (*Harper's Bazaar*)

Quick fix: in the second sentence, insert *had* before *cofounded*.

Writers sometimes also forget to make a necessary downshift from the present-progressive tense to the present-perfect tense.

 China is slowing down, but the buildings keep going up—until now. (*New York Times*)

 China is slowing down, but the buildings have kept going up—until now. [The phrase *is slowing down* is in the present-progressive; *have kept going up* is in the present-perfect.]

Writers sometimes also neglect to make a downshift in a midsentence or sentence-ending participial phrase.

 ...Carl Osborne and his family have been tenants for two years, moving in after the previous owner lost the house in a foreclosure. (*New York Times*)

 ...Carl Osborne and his family have been tenants for two years, having moved in after the previous owner lost the house....

52 The Clumsily *Unsplit* Infinitive

The notion that under no circumstances should an infinitive (the word *to* followed by the stem of a verb) be split persists despite the fact that no editor or grammarian in her right mind has ever issued any such prohibition. True, many a split infinitive leaves a sentence looking tousled and sounding clunky, and any sentence of that sort can be rephrased easily enough.

 Google was the endpoint of this process: It may represent open systems and leveled architecture, but with superb irony and strategic brilliance it came to almost completely control that openness. (*Wired*)

 ...it came to control that openness almost completely. OR: ...it came to exert almost complete control over that openness.

Sometimes, though, a writer has so strenuously avoided splitting an infinitive that the result is painfully ungraceful.

 They [Neanderthals] did attend to corpses, if minimally. This, the authors offer, suggests...a need to separate physically the dead from the living.... (*New York Times*)

The phrasing *a need to separate physically the dead from the living* is avoidably maladroit. The first alternative is to split the infinitive for phrasing that's idiomatic and pleasing to the ear.

 ...a need to physically separate the dead from the living....

But the writer can also edit the infinitive out of the sentence.

This ... suggests ... a need to ensure that the dead were physically separated from the living. ...

 Sometimes, they are unable to analyze properly the data they collect. (*The Long Tail: Why the Future of Business Is Selling Less of More* [Hyperion], by Chris Anderson)

 Sometimes, they are unable to properly analyze the data they collect. OR: Sometimes, they cannot properly analyze the data they collect.

In sum, it's unwise to find fault with a split infinitive if the alternative is awkward phrasing. But remember that you always have the option of recasting the entire shebang of a sentence to ditch the infinitive.

53 *That* we can do without.

A sentence in which a verb of saying (such as *said* or *remarked*) or a verb of thinking or speculating (such as *knew* or *wondered*) is followed by phrasing in which an adverbial dependent clause is tucked inside a nominative dependent clause is always at risk of ending up with a surplus *that*.

 She knows that if a person is on the street that it's not necessarily due to laziness or drug addiction. (*The Fabulous Girl's Guide to Decorum* [Broadway Books], by Kim Izzo and Ceri Marsh)

The nominative clause in that sentence (functioning as the direct object of *knows*) is intended to be *that it's not necessarily due to laziness or drug addiction*. Whisk away the adverbial dependent clause (*if a person is on the street*) from the sentence, though, and you're left with the stuttery nonsense of *She knows that that it's not necessarily due to laziness or drug addiction,* in which the nominative dependent clause starts off with duplicate *thats* when one alone will do the trick.

The quickest fix? Substitute a comma for the second *that*.

 She knows that if a person is on the street, it's not necessarily due to laziness or drug addiction. OR [reworded]: She knows that a person living on the street isn't necessarily a lazybones or a drug addict.

54 *That* we do need.

A small but vocal minority of editors, enamored of the hyperconcise, would like to eject the word *that* from virtually all sentences in which it appears at the start of a nominative dependent clause. They insist that the word serves no purpose and clutters a sentence. But the deletion of *that* can diminish the readability of a sentence, as in this one about Bob Dylan:

 By now we know the voice—one of the most brilliant, peculiar and iconic instruments on Earth—is somewhat ravaged by the endless touring, smoking and what have you. (*Pittsburgh Post-Gazette*)

Reaching the verb *is*, after the second dash, a reader is likely to register a minor shock and realize that she's been misled about the direction the sentence has been taking her. *Earth*, after all, appears to be a likely place for the sentence to come to its end: *By now we know the voice—one of the most brilliant, peculiar, and iconic instruments on Earth*. The writer has failed to signal to the reader that *voice* is in fact not the direct object of the transitive verb, *know*, in the independent clause but instead the subject of a nominative dependent clause. That dependent clause, in its entirety, is the direct object of *know*, and the predicate of that clause makes an assertion about *voice*. The insertion of *that* at the start of the dependent clause will spare the reader a nanosecond of confusion.

By now we know that the voice—one of the most brilliant, peculiar, and iconic instruments on Earth—is somewhat ravaged....

Even more disorienting is the second sentence in the following excerpt, about a supermarket chain's policy of "locking" prices instead of gradually raising them.

Giant Eagle's first round of price locks officially was set to end Jan. 2. This time around, the company said it will guarantee prices on locked items won't change at least until spring.... (*Pittsburgh Post-Gazette*)

This time around, the company said it will guarantee that prices on locked items won't change at least until spring....

55 This rule is too vague.

Oh, so there's an acceptable degree of vagueness permissible in the phrasing of a rule? But beyond that degree, the phrasing becomes completely intolerable? That, sadly, is the line of thinking into which many readers will be forced when they encounter sentences like the following.

The Eastern European love poems translated by Friedrich Daumer are too mediocre to merit attention.... (*New York Times*)

Of course the precise intellectual and social history of bad economic practices is too useless to study.... (*New York Times*)

It's in the best interest of logic, clarity, and the reader's well-being to avoid the adverb *too* when the adjective following it denotes a quality that's wholly undesirable. *Too* works perfectly fine, though, in sentences in which the adjective is neutral (*That restaurant is too expensive for me*) or positive (*She is too smart for me*).

Some other events ... are considered too worthless to write about. (*New York Times*)

Some other events ... are considered unworthy of coverage.

56 I've had my car broken into twice this year.

Not really—I didn't *arrange* for the break-ins. What possessed me, then, to write such a silly sentence?

I'm not alone, though.

 Adam Sandler Reportedly Had Several Native American Actors Walk Off the Set of His Netflix Movie (headline, *New York*'s vulture.com)

 I have had cousins, friends and church members shot and killed. (*Pittsburgh Post-Gazette*)

The writer of that second sentence, which appeared in an op-ed essay, is the pastor of a church, not some lowlife fessing up to a slew of murders.

Grammarians have a name for this regrettable use of *had*. They call it the passive causative *had*. It's perfectly ducky in sentences such as *She had her driveway resurfaced* and *She had her car repaired,* in which the action is positive, restorative, remedial. But when the action is burglarious or destructive, and when a sentence seems to be saying that a person has gone out of her way to wreak havoc on herself (or on someone or something else), it's time to rephrase. At the very least, the writer can substitute a form of the verb *to be* for *had: Her iPad was stolen,* instead of *She had her iPad stolen.* In sum, resort to the passive causative *had* only when the news is good, or at least neutral.

57 Just because other writers write sentences like this doesn't mean you have to.

 Just because something increases your metabolic rate doesn't mean it's good for you. (*New York Times*)

That common sentence pattern sounds conversational, and it's fine if your context is the equivalent of a casual Friday at work. But the pattern is otherwise messy, even crass—because it forces an adverbial dependent clause (the word-group beginning with *just because*) to serve as the subject of a sentence. That's a grammatically unnatural act for a member of the adverb family to commit, because the subject of a sentence must be a noun or the equivalent of a noun—namely, a pronoun, a nominative dependent clause, or an adjective preceded by the article *the* (such as *the underemployed*).

A reliable quick fix is to substitute *the fact that* for *just because*—a maneuver that transforms an adverbial dependent clause into a nominative dependent clause.

 The fact that something increases your metabolic rate doesn't mean it's good for you.

Often, though, it's better to rephrase the sentence.

 Not everything that increases your metabolic rate is necessarily good for you.

58. A middle-aged incompetent, the author and his best friend lament the error in this sentence.

The lamentable error in the sentence flaunting itself as the title of this chapter is what we might call overshared phrasing. Although the phrase *a middle-aged incompetent* is obviously intended to provide information about only one person, it's in the unenviable position of being shared by the two parts of the subject: both *author* and *friend*. The result is a violation of syntactic etiquette. A sentence that begins with an appositive expressed in the singular can correctly be followed only by a subject expressed in the singular. The easiest way to repair the title sentence is to reposition the appositive: *The author (a middle-aged incompetent) and his best friend have nothing to lament about the grammar in this revision.*

Beware, then, of phrasing in which an additive-compound subject (a subject taking the form of *A and B* or of *A, B, and C*) is preceded by a prepositional phrase, a participial phrase, an appositive, or some other sort of introductory element whose purpose is to describe only the first member of the subject. That introductory phrase will inevitably appear to be describing the one or more additional members of the subject as well.

 A native of north India and the father of two boys, ages 7 and 9, Mr. Singh and his wife, Manjit Kaur, were inspired to open a straightforward Indian restaurant.... (*Pittsburgh Post-Gazette*)

Mr. Singh alone is the father of the two boys.

 A native of north India and the father of two boys, ages 7 and 9, Mr. Singh, along with his wife, Manjit Kaur, was inspired to open a straightforward Indian restaurant....

 A herky-jerky jackanapes who triumphed over naysayers as the host of NBC's *Late Night with Conan O'Brien*, O'Brien and company delighted dormitories across America.... (*Critical Mass: Four Decades of Essays, Reviews, Hand Grenades, and Hurrahs* [Doubleday], by James Wolcott)

The appositive is the exclusive property of O'Brien alone and cannot be shared with *company*.

 A herky-jerky jackanapes who triumphed over naysayers as the host of NBC's *Late Night with Conan O'Brien*, O'Brien led a loopy crew that delighted dormitories across America....

The Comma-ist Manifesto

59 Unsuitable Attachments

It's easy to forget what a difference a comma can make in a sentence, especially a compound sentence. A compound sentence gets its name from the fact that it's compounded of at least two independent clauses, which we can think of as miniature sentences—word-groups that could stand on their own as grammatically complete statements. In a compound sentence, the two miniature sentences are often hitched together by a coordinating conjunction, a word such as *and*. *And* is the consummate coupler—it's forever tugging two things together. The trouble is that those two things sometimes get a little too close when in fact they don't belong together at all, and their relationship can start to look unseemly. It's in everybody's best interest to pry the two things apart, so that people don't get the wrong idea. And that's where the comma comes in.

Rumours of Nick's use of heroin persisted long after his death and the 'heroin chic' of the nineties saw them gain even more ground. (*Nick Drake* [Bloomsbury], by Patrick Humphries) [Note the British spelling and the British single quotation marks.]

Look at what *and* is up to in that sentence. At first, it seems to be joining *death* and *"heroin chic."* But then we read further and realize we've been misled. The compound noun *"heroin chic"* isn't the second object of the preposition *after*; that preposition in fact has only one object: *death*. And *"heroin chic,"* as it turns out, is the subject of the second independent clause of the sentence. But how were we expected to know that without having been tipped off? The sentence needs a barrier between the two independent clauses so that we immediately know when one has ended and the second one has begun. A comma would be the perfect boundary-marker.

Another kind of unsuitable attachment is that in which the subject of a sentence-ending independent clause can be mistaken for the direct object of a verb at the end of an introductory adverbial dependent clause. That is, a reader initially misconstrues an intransitive verb as a transitive verb. (This problem afflicting some complex sentences, which by definition consist of one independent clause and one or more dependent clauses, is treated in Chapter 60.) A comma between *driving* and *everyone* in the following sentence will resolve the problem.

When Robbie the Robot is driving everyone will also have more time for work and social networking and watching YouTube. (*Wall Street Journal*)

Unsuitable attachments can take other forms. In the following sentence, the conjunction *and* appears to be joining the two participial phrases following *while* at the end of the first independent clause, but the second participial phrase needs to be understood as a lead-in to the second independent clause.

 The main problem was that [Moe] Tucker liked to play drums while standing up and being pregnant, she couldn't physically reach to play them properly. (*Seeing the Light: Inside the Velvet Underground* [St. Martin's Press], by Rob Jovanovic)

Quick fixes: insert a comma before *and*, or insert commas both before and after *and*.

In the next specimen, the conjunction *and* seems to be uniting two adverbial dependent clauses that follow the first independent clause, but readers need to grasp that the second adverbial dependent clause belongs to the second independent clause. A comma before *and* will prevent misreading.

 They only spoke when it was absolutely necessary and when Reed later needed support, it wasn't forthcoming from Morrison. (*Seeing the Light: Inside the Velvet Underground* [St. Martin's Press], by Rob Jovanovic) [For a discussion of the positioning of modifiers like *only*, see Chapter 22.]

60 After I ate my mind cleared up.

A mind is a terrible thing to taste. So why mislead your readers into thinking—before the poor dears have reached the end of your sentence—that you've been gorging on gray matter? Spare them. A comma should follow an introductory adverbial dependent clause (such as *After I ate*)—especially if, as in the title of this chapter, the dependent clause ends with a verb. The subject of the independent clause of the sentence, after all, could initially be misconstrued as the object of that verb.

Too often, though, writers don't trouble themselves with the comma—and end up troubling the reader.

 When we leave my friend gives me a loaf of his good bread. (*Aftermath: On Marriage and Separation* [Farrar, Straus and Giroux], by Rachel Cusk)

 When we leave, my friend gives me a loaf....

When an adverbial dependent clause appears not at the beginning of a sentence but instead after an independent clause in a compound-complex sentence, which comprises two or more independent clauses and at least one dependent clause, the omission of a comma can be just as jarring.

 I was supposed to meet Chiocchio on the fifth floor of the main building, but when I arrived there was no receptionist, no security to speak of, no one I could find to ask where he was. (*New Yorker*)

On her first way through the sentence, many a reader cannot help regarding *there* as an adverb modifying *arrived* in an adverbial dependent clause (*when I arrived there*), but when she reaches the next word, the verb *was*, she realizes that the writer intended for her to read *there* as an expletive, as the structural prop with which the second independent clause of the sentence begins. So why not do the reader the favor of inserting a comma after *arrived*?

Even when such a sentence isn't practically pleading for misinterpretation, every reader is on principle entitled to a comma after an introductory adverbial dependent clause. The reader is also entitled to punctuational consistency when a sentence split into halves by a semicolon includes two such introductory clauses.

When he is outdoors, he wears a tweed cap; when he is indoors he pushes his half-glasses up on top of his head. (*New Yorker*)

61 In Your Infinitive Wisdom

An infinitive or an infinitive phrase that is positioned at the beginning of a sentence as an introductory element should always be followed by a comma. To omit the comma is to invite misreading.

A couple of definitions are in order. An infinitive consists of the combination of the word *to* and the stem of a verb; *to write* is an infinitive. The word *to* in an infinitive is not a preposition. (Grammarians refer to it variously as the sign of the infinitive, the infinitive marker, and the infinitival particle.) An infinitive phrase consists of an infinitive and any objects and modifiers it has attracted to itself. *To write a sentence without errors* is an infinitive phrase.

When an infinitive is set out at the start of a sentence, writers sometimes forget to insert a comma after it.

To survive Walton had to get moving, either to expand his chain of Ben Franklin stores or to begin a new discount operation. (*The Retail Revolution: How Wal-Mart Created a Brave New World of Business* [Picador], by Nelson Lichtenstein)

Walton can initially be misconstrued as the object of *to survive* instead of being instantly recognized as the subject of the independent clause. The solution? Insert a comma after *survive*.

An unpunctuated introductory infinitive phrase can cause trouble as well.

[about a gossip columnist] Janet's weekly spread eats up large quantities of dish: to feed the supply she relies heavily on a somewhat creepy tactic that she calls "befriending the innocents." (*Wacky Chicks: Life Lessons from Fearlessly Inappropriate and Fabulously Eccentric Women* [Simon & Schuster], by Simon Doonan)

Readers can easily mistake the phrasing *she relies heavily on* for an adjectival dependent clause (with an implied *that* at its head) modifying *supply*. But readers need to know at the outset that *she* is the subject of the second independent clause in the sentence. The solution? Insert a comma after *supply*.

Now have another look at the second sentence in the paragraph that starts off this chapter—a sentence that includes two infinitive phrases. Why is there no comma after

To omit the comma at the beginning of the sentence? Simple: that infinitive phrase is functioning as the complete subject of the sentence, not as an introductory element. In contrast, consider this sentence: *To prevent misreading, a good writer always inserts a comma after an introductory infinitive phrase.* There, *To prevent misreading* is an introductory infinitive phrase.

62 A Crash Course in the Punctuation of Introductory Prepositional Phrases

If a short unpunctuated introductory prepositional phrase (or even a pair or trio of such phrases) is unlikely to cause confusion by blurring the boundary between itself and the subject of the sentence, there's no pressing need for a comma to follow the prepositional phrase (or phrases). But if a reader cannot instantly discern the grammatical status of the word following the introductory prepositional phrase, you are paying her a courtesy by inserting a comma at the end of the phrase.

 For most fans attending a baseball game is a summer diversion, an addiction, an act of devotion. (*New York Times*)

Before reaching the verb *is*, a reader can easily misconstrue *attending* as a participle (and the phrase *attending a baseball game* as a participial phrase modifying *fans*). But she needs to know from the outset that *attending* is a gerund—and the subject of the sentence. The solution? Insert a comma after *fans*.

63 Independent Versus Dependent Adjectives

Whenever two or more consecutive adjectives precede a noun, you need to decide whether a comma should separate them. Your intuition usually does the work for you: it's unlikely that you would insert a comma between *same* and *realistic* in *They each have the same realistic outlook*; and you probably wouldn't have to think twice about the need for a comma between *unshowered* and *overtalkative* in *For the return flight, I was stuck next to an unshowered, overtalkative teenager.*

Even professional writers, however, sometimes mishandle the punctuation of consecutive adjectives. The following sentence includes four such pairs. How many commas would you add?

 Peanuts is [a] short frail man with big blue eyes, sparse white hair and a fair smooth complexion. (*New York Observer*)

If you added two (one after *short* and one after *fair*), you have a sure sense of when a comma is called for. And the foolproof strategy for determining whether or not a comma must separate two adjectives isn't complicated. All you need to do is ask yourself two questions.

First, if you were to wedge the coordinating conjunction *and* between the two adjectives, would the phrasing sound perfectly natural to your ears? If it would, insert a comma. If it wouldn't, leave the phrasing alone.

Second, if you reversed the two adjectives, would the phrasing also sound fine? If it would, you need a comma. If it would not, don't add a comma.

If we apply those two rules to the sentence above, it's obvious, for instance, that *fair and smooth complexion* and *smooth, fair complexion* sound entirely natural but that *big and blue eyes* and *blue big eyes* do not.

In the first instance, the adjectives *fair* and *smooth* are independently describing *complexion*. Think of them as loner adjectives. (Grammarians call them coordinate adjectives.) Adjectives that like to keep to themselves deserve a comma between them.

In the second instance, though, the writer means that Peanuts's blue eyes also happen to be big. *Big* isn't so much modifying *eyes* as limiting and refining the meaning of the phrase *blue eyes*. It's as if *big* is leaning on *blue* in the phrasing; one of the adjectives is dependent on the other, so they shouldn't be separated punctuationally. (Grammarians call them cumulative adjectives.)

A writer's failure to separate independent adjectives with a comma can easily give readers the wrong idea.

 Her fifth self-titled album, released in surprise form late last week, is a collection of songs that highlight Beyoncé's evolution as a woman and [an] artist. (huffingtonpost.com)

The writer of that sentence untroubledly tells the reader—who may or may not have been following the recording career of Beyoncé—that the singer has released five albums entitled simply *Beyoncé*. The problem, however, is that only one of her albums, her fifth, bears that title. The writer needs to make it clear to readers that the album discussed in the sentence is the singer's fifth album and that it just happens to be self-titled. Each adjective—*fifth* and *self-titled*—should be independently modifying the noun *album*, so a comma must separate the two.

64 Let's get serious about the serial comma.

The omission of what grammarians call the serial comma—the comma preceding the coordinating conjunction *and* in a series of three or more elements—is standard editorial practice at American newspapers, some magazines, and some book publishers. But the omission is difficult to justify and will not be tolerated here, because it too often results in misreadable sentences—and sometimes perplexing ones as well.

The source of the trouble is that the coordinating conjunction *and*, if not preceded by a comma, unites the second-last and final elements of the series into an inseparable couple—even when that is not the writer's intention.

 Happy clips from everyday life—a father bathing with his baby, a grandfather playing piano with his granddaughter and a teacher playing with her students—are seen during the spot.... (*New York Times*)

Without a comma separating *granddaughter* from *and*, readers can initially misread *teacher* as the second object of the preposition *with*—and therefore conclude that the grandfather is playing piano with both his granddaughter and a teacher.

 She pushed aside a bottle of sparkling water, a glass with a silver straw and a delicate orchid placed before her and spoke frankly about her plans. (*New York Times*)

The lack of a comma after *straw* at first suggests that the glass not only has been handsomely set before the guest with an elegant straw bobbing in it but also has been festooned with an orchid.

In the following specimen, the elements in a three-part series are independent clauses, but without a comma before *and*, the subject of the third independent clause at first appears to be a second object of the preposition in the prepositional phrase at the end of the second independent clause. A comma before *and* will prevent misreading.

 You eat a lot of takeout, your kids holler for Nikes and the TV is on five hours a day. (*Culture Jam: How to Reverse America's Suicidal Consumer Binge—and Why We Must* [Quill], by Kalle Lasn)

When a reader is accustomed to seeing the *a, b and c* pattern for a series, it's easy for her to misread a sentence such as the following, in which the *a, b and c* phrasing in the predicate isn't intended to be read as a series. Instead, *b and c* form a pair of words elaborating on what is meant by *a*.

 The burger itself—made of brisket, short rib and sirloin—was excellent, tender and juicy. (*Pittsburgh City Paper*)

The writer is not saying three things about the hamburger—that it was excellent, it was tender, and it was juicy. What the writer is saying is that the hamburger was excellent *because* it was tender and juicy. Of course, the sentence could be rephrased so that a reader won't discern a series where none was intended: *The burger itself—made of brisket, short rib, and sirloin—was excellent, both tender and juicy.*

65 Fusspot Punctuation: Dates and Place-Names

When you're presenting a date in the standard sequence of month, day, and year, don't forget to insert a comma after the year.

 There they were on *New York* magazine's February 5, 1973 cover.... (*Holy Terror: Andy Warhol Up Close* [HarperCollins], by Bob Colacello)

Quick fix: ... *New York* magazine's February 5, 1973, cover....

When you're presenting a place-name in the form of town or city and state, town or city and county, or town or city and country, don't forget to insert a comma after the name of the state, county, or country.

 The Alpine in North Conway, New Hampshire was a bar with a small stage.... (*Seeing the Light: Inside the Velvet Underground* [St. Martin's Press], by Rob Jovanovic)

Quick fix: The Alpine in North Conway, New Hampshire, was a bar....

If the name of the state, county, or country is immediately followed by a participle, the second comma is omitted, and a hyphen unites the participle with the second half of the place-name: *She has worked for the Dallas, Texas-based company since 2011.*

66 Throwaway and Must-Have Appositives

Each comma we insert into a sentence is in fact making a cut, an incision. Knowing when and where to make such cuts—as well as knowing what in a sentence is cuttable—is a hallmark of the skilled writer.

The most subtle errors in the usage of the comma—errors that ultimately lead to misreading—are often the result of the writer's failure to preserve the distinction between information that is essential to a sentence and information that is not essential. Such errors are so pervasive that the discussion will consume ten chapters.

Before we concern ourselves with terminology, let's have a look at two pairs of sentences identical in their phrasing but different in their punctuation—and, more important, different in what they say. Can you discern the differences in meaning?

1a. Mina's daughter Kelly and her son Jason are attending college.

1b. Mina's daughter, Kelly, and her son, Jason, are attending college.

2a. Annie Wright's novel *Celestialities* was published in 2014.

2b. Annie Wright's novel, *Celestialities,* was published in 2014.

In the first pair, one sentence tells us that Mina has only one daughter and only one son, and the other tells us that Mina has at least two daughters and at least two sons. Can you tell which is which? And can you tell which of the sentences in the second pair declares that Annie Wright has published only one novel?

If you've concluded that sentence 1a is the sentence asserting that Mina has more than one daughter and more than one son, and if you've concluded that sentence 2b asserts that Annie Wright has published only one novel, you obviously have a strong grasp of how the presence or absence of commas makes a profound difference in the meaning that a sentence transmits to a reader. And that difference has everything to do with the distinction between essential and nonessential elements.

An essential element is a must-have. It's indispensable. It can't be cut. A sentence cannot accurately communicate its intended meaning unless the must-have element is in place. What the must-have element does is set limits on the meaning of the word or words directly preceding it. (That's why such an element is also called a restrictive or defining element.) The must-have element typically specifies a subset of a larger set of people or things. That way, the reader knows that the writer is discussing not the larger set but only a smaller part of it. *Must-have elements are never set off with any punctuation.* Sentence 1a lacks commas around the names of the two children because the names Kelly and Jason are needed to specify which daughter and which son are attending college. The names restrict or narrow the scope or range of the meaning of the preceding nouns *daughter* and *son*. Putting commas around the two names would signal to the reader that the names aren't needed and can be cut away from the body of the sentence, but those two names are in fact crucial to the sentence's meaning.

A nonessential element, in contrast, provides information that a sentence could easily do without—but the information has been included for the reader as a little something extra, a bonus, a present. Consider it a throwaway. The writer has had no obligation or responsibility to provide it, but she has bestowed it upon the reader in a spirit of generosity. The reader can either take it or leave it. *Throwaway elements must always be set off with punctuation—most often with commas, though dashes or parentheses can also do the trick.* The commas around the names of the two children in sentence 1b and around the title of the novel in sentence 2b signal to the reader that the information presented between commas isn't vital to the reader's understanding. Both sentences will still accurately convey their meanings even if the information set off with commas has been cut out.

The nouns *Kelly, Jason,* and *Celestialities* in the sample sentences above are classified as appositives. An appositive is a noun or a noun phrase that immediately follows, and provides information about, a noun. (The word *appositive* literally means "positioned right next to.") A writer is responsible for determining whether an appositive in a sentence is a must-have or a throwaway—and she must then punctuate the appositive appropriately so that the reader can instantly grasp the intended meaning.

An alert reader sometimes has no trouble recognizing from the context that an appositive has been mispunctuated.

Over time, Arturo and I became friendly, exchanging confidences about our kids—we both had a boy and a girl, his daughter Hillary named admiringly after Mrs. Clinton, while his son, Bryan Armany, like mine, Luke Auden, had a first name he liked the sound of and the middle name of an artist he admired. (*New Yorker*)

Since we've been told that the writer and Arturo each have one son and one daughter, the appositive *Hillary* in the phrasing *his daughter Hillary* needs commas at both ends—because one of Arturo's daughters is not being distinguished from another daughter of his. And, no, the writer's daughter isn't also named Hillary. (The sentence suffers as well from faulty parallelism; see Chapter 41.)

A reader is at a disadvantage, though, when encountering a passage like the following.

[Robert] Putnam, the author of "Bowling Alone," is the director of the Saguaro Seminar for civic engagement at Harvard's Kennedy School of Government; [Jennifer M.] Silva, a sociologist, has been a postdoctoral fellow there. In her 2013 book "Coming Up Short: Working-Class Adulthood in an Age of Uncertainty" (Oxford), Silva reported the results of interviews she conducted with a hundred working-class adults in Lowell, Massachusetts and Richmond, Virginia, described her account of the structural inequalities that shape their lives as "a story of institutions—not individuals or their families," and argued that those inequalities are the consequence of the past half century's "massive effort to roll back social protections from the market." (*New Yorker*)

The absence of commas around the title of Silva's book leads a reader to conclude that Silva published more than one book in 2013 and that one of them is being distinguished from at least one other. A reader naturally wants to trust a magazine like *The New Yorker,* but a quick Internet search turns up Silva's curriculum vitae, and within seconds a reader learns not only that Silva published just one book in 2013 but also that in her career thus far (by mid-2015) she has published no other books. The sentence therefore misinforms readers about Silva's book-publication history. (The writer has also mispunctuated a place-name; see Chapter 65.)

 In her book, "Coming Up Short: Working-Class Adulthood in an Age of Uncertainty" (Oxford, 2013), Silva reported the results of interviews she conducted with a hundred working-class adults in Lowell, Massachusetts, and Richmond, Virginia....

 A lot of it [the production of the ballet *The Red Detachment of Women*] is camp—a vein tapped by Mark Morris in the version he made for John Adams's 1987 opera "Nixon in China." (*New Yorker*)

Adams's many works include only one opera from 1987. A comma must therefore follow *opera*.

Following are two more punctuationally troubled sentences, the first from the review of a CD.

 "No need for a compliment / I can pat myself on the back," he sings on the album closer "Form of Flattery." (*New York Times*)

Since when can an album have more than one closer—that is, more than one final song? The title of the song identified as the closer is a throwaway appositive; a comma must precede it.

 Next year will note the fortieth anniversary of his debut novel *The Rachel Papers,* a brilliant showpiece of young-man bravado.... (*Critical Mass: Four Decades of Essays, Reviews, Hand Grenades, and Hurrahs* [Doubleday], by James Wolcott)

A writer can have only one debut novel; its title is a throwaway appositive. A comma must follow *novel*.

Sometimes a must-have appositive is mistakenly punctuated as if it were a throwaway.

 Louise called Hemingway "that bloodiest of all killers," but preferred his writing to that of his friend, Gertrude Stein. (*Louise Brooks* [Knopf], by Barry Paris)

Gertrude Stein wasn't Hemingway's only friend, and thus her name is not a throwaway appositive. The comma preceding *Gertrude* must vanish.

67 Throwaway and Must-Have Quotations Functioning as Appositives

Quotations included within a sentence often function as appositives, and therefore they can be either nonessential or essential, throwaways or must-haves. It's easy to determine whether a quotation is essential to a sentence. In the sentence *Morrissey's song "Come Back to Camden" ends with the words "I'll be good,"* the quotation *"I'll be good"* is obviously essential—because without the quotation, the sentence would look and sound unfinished. A reader would justifiably (and exasperatedly) ask, *"Which words?"* A comma before the quotation would therefore be disastrous; the comma would misleadingly imply that the quotation that follows it is disposable. But in the sentence *In 1974, Burger King introduced a new advertising slogan, "Have it your way,"* the quotation is nonessential— because the sentence would make perfect sense without it. The quotation *"Have it your way"* is merely supplementary information, and thus a comma needs to precede it.

When the article *the* precedes the noun to which a quotational appositive is annexed, the appositive is almost always a must-have; and whenever it is a must-have, it must not be set off punctuationally. When the article *a* or *an* precedes the noun, however, the quotational appositive is certain to be a throwaway and must be set off punctuationally. Quotations functioning as must-have appositives, unfortunately, are frequently punctuated as if they were throwaways. In each of the following sentences, the comma inserted before the appositive must be deleted.

 Not long ago, *Rolling Stone* ran a cover photograph of a pouty, surly Jim Morrison with the headline, "He's hot, he's sexy, and he's dead." (*Critical Mass: Four Decades of Essays, Reviews, Hand Grenades, and Hurrahs* [Doubleday], by James Wolcott)

 The spokesman did not cite the classic Marx Brothers line, "Who are you going to believe, me or your own eyes?" (*Wall Street Journal*)

 This is the restaurant that finally answers the question, "What if we set lobster fra diavolo on fire?" (*New York Times*)

68 This sentence about my close friend and colleague the talk-show host Amelia Samson needs to be comma-free.

Many of us, though, are itching to cram commas into crannies where they don't belong. Maybe it's because a misguided English teacher once insisted that we pop a comma in wherever we would pause if we were reading a sentence aloud. Uncalled-for commas, though, often distort the meaning of a sentence.

 When his friend, the painter Denis Wirth-Miller, told him that Muybridge's *Studies for the Human Figure in Motion*, made in 1872-85, could be seen at the Victoria and Albert Museum, close to where he lived, Bacon had ample opportunity to borrow the images. (*The Gilded Gutter Life of Francis Bacon* [Pantheon], by Daniel Farson)

Francis Bacon had more than one friend in his long life. The commas following *friend* and *Wirth-Miller* need to be dispatched into oblivion.

Sometimes writers get into punctuational trouble when they omit the article *the* before the second element of a multipart appositive.

 [Jimmy] Kimmel's friend, sports columnist Bill Simmons, sees a hard-wired ambition. (*Rolling Stone*)

 Kimmel's friend the sports columnist Bill Simmons sees a hardwired ambition.

To return to the sentence at the head of this chapter, a sentence certain to tempt many a writer to poke commas into its phrasing: *Amelia Samson* specifies *which* talk-show host the writer means; the phrase *the talk-show host* specifies *which* close friend and colleague the writer means. Every word and phrase in the sentence is essential to a reader's understanding. Using commas to set off any of those phrases would be the equivalent of scissoring the phrases out of the sentence—depriving us readers of information crucial to our knowing exactly which person the writer is bringing to our attention.

69 That Bane of Grammarians the Inspissated Plentitive

Why are so many writers quick to stick in a comma after *grammarians* in a phrase like that, just as they were hell-bent on shoving in the commas that are boldfaced and bracketed in the excerpts below?

 [about the poet John Ashbery] He's already been compared to Hart Crane by that dashing old blowhard[,] Harold Bloom, who will compare anyone to Crane at the drop of a hat. (*New Criterion*)

 Mention [George] Clooney, and the subject turns next to whether (or to what extent) he's the modern version of that touchstone of male charm[,] Cary Grant. (*The Atlantic*)

The writers of those sentences dreamily expect us to believe that in all of humankind, there has been one and only one dashing old blowhard, one and only one touchstone of male charm.

The erring, bracketed commas need to vaporize a.s.a.p.—because in each case the noun following the initial comma is specifying which *one* of the dashing old blowhards or which *one* of the touchstones of male charm the writer has in mind. Those nouns have a limiting, particularizing function: each offers the reader a serving of information without which the full meal of the sentence would be missing an important dish. That noun (discussed elsewhere as a must-have appositive [see Chapter 66]) rounds out the repast and can't be cut from the menu. But the bracketed commas in those sentences are, in effect, swiping food from our plates.

How delightful it is, then, to see someone get things right, as Rachel Cusk (or her editor) does in this sentence—for there is surely more than one sort of *silly complicit creature*:

 The feminist scorns that silly complicit creature the housewife. (*Aftermath: On Marriage and Separation* [Farrar, Straus and Giroux])

It's possible, though, to write a sentence in which the kind of comma being decried in this chapter can in fact be justified.

 And last week it happened in that exemplar of editing excellence, The New Yorker. (boston.com)

If a writer truly does believe that *The New Yorker* is the one and only exemplar of editing excellence, the comma has every reason to stay put.

There's another species of sentence, though, that's even more disconcerting.

 But it took 240 years before our fair city could enjoy that most exquisite of French delicacies[,] the beignet. (*St. Louis Homes and Lifestyles*)

Granted, that bracketed, boldfaced comma might at first look perfectly plausible. After all, how can there be more than one "most exquisite of French delicacies"? And if there's only one, then there's no pressing need to name it; the writer can assume that any informed reader will already know what it is. The noun or noun phrase (the appositive, again, to be technical about things) trailing after the comma thus looks disposable, like any other nonessential appositive. But then you suddenly realize that the sentence is expressing not a fact but a judgment—an assessment by its very nature subjective, not universal. Who's to say what the most exquisite of French delicacies truly is? All we're getting from the sentence is the writer's opinion.

It turns out that there's a very easy way to determine that the comma in such a sentence deserves the bum's rush. If the noun or noun phrase after the comma had been subtracted and replaced with a blank before you ever took a gander at the sentence, would you have been able to fill in the blank with the very same noun or noun phrase that the writer had tendered? No? Then the information presented in the noun or noun phrase was obviously central to the meaning of the sentence. It was a must-have appositive. It thus cannot be set off with a comma.

A colon or a dash, however, is permissible to set off the two types of sentence-ending phrasing discussed in this chapter. Unlike the comma, which by its very nature is a scythe, cutting away what follows it (see Chapters 66-68 and 70-75), the colon serves as a gateway to clarifying phrasing (see Chapter 82), and a dash, like a writer's index finger, helpfully points the reader toward what she needs.

And thus we arrive at that most eagerly awaited of revelations: the fact that there's no such thing as an inspissated plentitive.

70 Throwaway and Must-Have Prepositional Phrases

Some writers and editors are criticized for punctuational overkill—especially the use of commas to set off certain prepositional phrases. *The New Yorker*, for instance, would insert the commas that are boldfaced and bracketed in the sentences below—commas that didn't appear in the periodicals and book from which the sentences are excerpted.

1. Another piece of classic Old New York will disappear tomorrow when the venerable hamburger paradise Prime Burger[**,**] at 5 E. 51st St.[**,**] will fire up the grill for the last time. (*New York Post*) [A comma is also needed after *tomorrow*; see Chapter 73.]
2. Nancy's second marriage[**,**] to the writer and Hellenophile Kevin Andrews[**,**] was, like her first, troubled. (*Wall Street Journal*)
3. Since getting divorced[**,**] in 2007, [Larry] David has lived a comfortable but not overly lavish or complicated existence.... (*New York*)
4. He played Hamlet in one of his final roles as a student, in a production that traveled to the Baryshnikov Arts Center[**,**] in New York. (*New York*)
5. [Joseph] Mitchell's output slowed after *The New Yorker* published the final installment of the Mr. Flood profile[**,**] in August 1945. (*New Republic*)
6. Pointing at [Robert] Sherwood, who had recently won a second Pulitzer Prize[**,**] for his drama *Idiot's Delight*, he [Robert Benchley] cringed in horror and cried out, "Those eyes—I can't stand those eyes looking at me...." (*Dorothy Parker: What Fresh Hell Is This?* [Penguin], by Marion Meade)

The need for the added commas becomes apparent when you start thinking about the implications of those sentences. If the bracketed commas were evicted from the first sentence, the prepositional phrase *at 5 E. 51st St.* would be forced, misleadingly, into a restrictive capacity—distinguishing one Prime Burger restaurant from one or more other Prime Burger restaurants situated elsewhere in the city or beyond. But Prime Burger was not part of a chain. The East Fifty-first Street Prime Burger was the one and only Prime Burger in existence. The details about its location were thus not essential to the sentence; they were merely value added. Like any other throwaway element (discussed in Chapters 66-69 and 71-75), therefore, the prepositional phrase needs to be set off with punctuation. And in this instance, the insertion of the two commas will ensure the accuracy of the sentence: an attentive reader will instantly know that Prime Burger had no sister restaurants.

So have another look at the other numbered sentences at the start of this chapter. (2) Without the added commas, the sentence about Nancy (the poet E. E. Cummings's only child) implies that she married the same man twice—but her first marriage was in fact to someone else (one of Theodore Roosevelt's grandsons). The prepositional phrase *to the writer and Hellenophile Kevin Andrews* is therefore a throwaway. (3) The writer and actor Larry David has been divorced only once, so the information about the year in which the divorce was granted is throwaway information. Omitting the comma before *in 2007* will misinform any alert reader about David's history of divorce. (4) It so happens that on this planet there is one and only one Baryshnikov

Arts Center. The fact that it happens to be in New York is a nonessential detail. (5) *The New Yorker* published the final installment of Joseph Mitchell's series about Old Mr. Flood only once. A reader doesn't absolutely need to know in which year the piece was published. (6) A writer can be awarded a second Pulitzer Prize only once. The prepositional phrase specifying the title of the play for which Sherwood was honored with the second prize is a throwaway.

In each sentence with corrected punctuation, a prepositional phrase that is not intended to distinguish one thing or person from another is no longer being forced into seeming to do so. Unpunctuated prepositional phrases that provide merely nonessential information can distract, puzzle, or mislead a reader.

71 Throwaway and Must-Have Participial Phrases

A participial phrase is a parcel of verbal matter that begins with a participle and performs exactly like a single-word adjective. A participle is often defined as an adjective derived from a verb. There are two types of participles: the present participle, which always ends in *ing*, such as *exciting*; and the past participle, which usually ends in *ed* or *d*, such as *delighted* and *excited*, but sometimes has an irregular ending, as in *broken*.

A participial phrase comprises a present or past participle and other words attached to it. Examples are *walking to work* and *excited about the new job*. Such phrases might appear at the beginning of a sentence, at the end, or anywhere in between.

An introductory participial phrase must always be followed by a comma.

 Placed in a tight row they form the show's one instance of physical perfection.... (*New York Times*)

Quick fix: insert a comma after *row*.

Whether a participial phrase positioned in the middle of a sentence is set off with a pair of commas (or a pair of dashes or parentheses) depends on whether it is essential or nonessential. A nonessential, or throwaway, participial phrase requires punctuation—and the phrase must be set off at both ends. Such phrasing is not crucial to the meaning of the sentence. If, however, the participial phrase is a must-have (that is, if the meaning of the sentence would change if the participial phrase were removed), it is never set off punctuationally.

 With only days to go before the deadline to raise the debt limit or face national default, there are two plans on the table: the Reid plan endorsed by President Obama; and the Boehner plan, which Mr. Obama has suggested he would veto if it ever reaches his desk. (*New York Times*)

Although the independent clause tells a reader that only two plans are under consideration, the first phrase following the colon leads the attentive reader to the counterfactual conclusion that there are at least two Reid plans—only one of which has been endorsed by the president. The past-participial phrase *endorsed by President Obama*, in other words, is distinguishing one of Reid's plans from another; it's functioning as an essential modifier. But the writer has intended to make no such distinction; the writer wants the reader to understand that the two and only two plans under consideration are the Reid plan and the Boehner plan. A comma is therefore needed after *Reid plan*, so that a reader instantly knows that *endorsed by President Obama* is merely supplementary information, a throwaway—much as the adjectival dependent clause, beginning with *which*, at the end of the sentence is offering only supplementary information and is therefore set off with a comma.

Often, the information divulged in a midsentence participial phrase is disposable, and such a participial phrase needs to be set off punctuationally—not just at its front end but also at its rear. Writers often forget to insert the rear-end comma. The result is asymmetrical punctuation (see Chapter 80).

 He stepped down in 2005, complaining that the magazine business had become "conventional" and "business-driven" and now spends his days on various entrepreneurial and artistic ventures.... (*Wall Street Journal*)

Quick fix: insert a comma between the second *n* in *business-driven* and the closing quotation mark (*"business-driven,"*).

Finally, a participial phrase positioned at the end of a sentence is not preceded by a comma if it provides essential information. A sentence-ending participial phrase offering nonessential information, however, such as the phrase *done in his last years* in the following sentence, must have a comma before it.

 One of his least probing books is his most famous in English: his autobiography, "The World of Yesterday," a lusterless, chatty, hastily-put-together, complacent account of his life done in his last years. (*Wall Street Journal*)

72 Throwaway and Must-Have Adjectival Dependent Clauses

An adjectival dependent clause is a dependent clause that works the same way an everyday adjective does: it describes somebody or something (see Chapter 9). Such a clause usually begins with *who, whom, whose, that*, or *which*—but may begin with *when, where*, or *why*.

Why bother with the terminology? Because a writer needs to know whether an adjectival dependent clause is indispensable to the sentence in which she has inserted it or whether it does nothing more than add a bit of supplementary information that the sentence can just as well do without. In the former case, the meaning of the sentence will change if the clause is removed, and therefore the clause must not be set off punctuationally. In the latter case, the meaning of the sentence will remain the same if the clause is discarded, so the clause must be set off with punctuation. Such a clause is a throwaway, a freebie. As with any other variety of throwaway phrasing (discussed in Chapters 66-71 and 73-75), a reader can either take it or leave it.

In the sentence *Jayne married the woman whom she had lived with for three years in Park Slope,* the adjectival dependent clause is a must-have and therefore is not preceded by a comma: the reader needs to know who *the woman* is, and the adjectival dependent clause *whom she had lived with for three years in Park Slope* delivers the necessary details. (If stripped of its dependent clause, the sentence, coming out of the blue as *Jayne married the woman,* would strike readers as grammatically complete—it has a subject, a predicate verb, and a direct object—but informationally incomplete.) In the sentence *Jayne married Skylie Marr, who turned out to be a somniloquist,* however, the information in the adjectival dependent clause *who turned out to be a somniloquist* isn't vital to the reader's understanding of who it was that Jayne married. The dependent clause offers merely some bonus information (*Jayne married Skylie Marr* could stand alone as a sentence both grammatically and informationally complete), so the dependent clause needs to be preceded by a comma.

Writers sometimes forget to punctuate a throwaway adjectival dependent clause, and the result is a sentence that doesn't transmit the intended meaning.

He looks at his sleeping wife who wakes up and wants to know if something is wrong. (*New York Review of Books*)

In that sentence, Gore Vidal, criticizing a short story by John O'Hara, is inadvertently informing the reader that the man designated by the pronoun *He* has more than one sleeping wife. The sleeping wife that the man happens to be looking at is the one who wakes up and wants to know if something is wrong. Nothing even in the undercurrents of the story, however, suggests that the man is a bigamist. The adjectival dependent clause *who wakes up and wants to know if something is wrong* is therefore disposable—it's a throwaway. A comma must precede it.

Writers occasionally neglect to insert a comma before a throwaway adjectival dependent clause beginning with *where* or *when*. In the following excerpt, the writer first seems to be distinguishing one movie-industry California from another and then one Pacific Palisades from another. There is in fact only one such California and only one Pacific Palisades in that California. A comma should precede *where* in both sentences.

In the spring of 1955 John and Sister went to California where he had a deal with Twentieth Century-Fox.... They rented a house in Pacific Palisades where O'Hara did his movie work.... (*The O'Hara Concern: A Biography of John O'Hara* [Random House], by Matthew J. Bruccoli)

Throwaway adjectival dependent clauses beginning with *when* must also be set off with commas.

More than 50,000 [gas] stations have closed since 1991 when there were nearly 200,000 nationwide.... (*New York Times*)

Only one year has ever been designated as 1991 (A.D., that is). The writer has not intended to differentiate one 1991 (in which there were almost 200,000 gas stations in the United States) from some other 1991.

Quick fix: insert a comma before *when*.

Many adjectival dependent clauses begin with *that* or *which*; and although most editors urge writers to use *which* at the start of throwaway clauses and *that* at the start of must-have clauses, many writers, unfortunately, use the words interchangeably.

 It was easy to spot him: Storyboard [a dancer] has a broad smile, high-set cheekbones, and large, imploring eyes that he sometimes frames within thick-rimmed glasses or, if the mood strikes him, plastic 3-D shades pilfered from a movie theatre. (*New Yorker*)

Storyboard has only one set of eyes, but the adjectival dependent clause (with an adverbial dependent clause tucked inside it) *that he sometimes frames within thick-rimmed glasses or, if the mood strikes him, plastic 3-D shades pilfered from a movie theatre*, which is affixed to *eyes* without a comma, tells the reader that one of Storyboard's sets of eyes is being distinguished from at least one other set of his eyes. The adjectival dependent clause, then, is presented as if it were a must-have, but it needs to be offered as a throwaway.

 Storyboard has ... large, imploring eyes, which he sometimes frames within thick-rimmed glasses....

73 Throwaway and Must-Have Sentence-Ending Adverbial Dependent Clauses

Sentences that begin with an independent clause (a word-group that can stand on its own as a complete sentence) and end with an adverbial dependent clause present a punctuational challenge. An adverbial dependent clause is a clause that begins with a subordinating conjunction—such as *because, although, even though, though, if, unless, where, after, as, before, while, when, whenever, since,* and *until*—and cannot stand on its own as a sentence. Small wonder, then, that such a clause is called dependent: it needs an independent clause to lean on. Although (as in this very sentence) an introductory adverbial dependent clause must be followed by a comma (see Chapter 60), a sentence-ending adverbial dependent clause sometimes must have a comma before it, and sometimes it must not.

How to determine whether a comma is needed? Consider the following two sentences—each of which ends with an underlined adverbial dependent clause beginning with *even though*.

 She has always been interested in moviemaking, <u>even though she majored in physics</u>.

 She went out for a walk in nothing but a sleeveless dress <u>even though the snow was already falling heavily</u>.

The information provided by the adverbial dependent clause in the first sentence is not essential to the sentence and therefore is preceded by a comma. The fact that the woman majored in physics is disposable, take-it-or-leave-it information. The dependent clause is a throwaway.

In the second sentence, though, the reader needs the contents of the adverbial dependent clause to achieve a full understanding of the sentence's meaning. There is nothing remarkable about the decision of a woman wearing a sleeveless dress to go out for a walk. What's remarkable is that she is wearing nothing more during a snowstorm. The adverbial dependent clause, then, is providing must-have information—details that the reader can't do without. Such a clause must never be cut off from the independent clause with a comma. The sentence will not be informationally complete unless the independent clause and the dependent clause are presented unseparated by punctuation (as in the sentence you are right now reading).

In deciding whether to insert a comma before a sentence-ending adverbial dependent clause, then, think about the contents of that clause. If the information it includes is setting limits on the meaning of what's expressed in the independent clause, do not insert a comma. But if the adverbial dependent clause provides merely supplementary information, punctuate it as a throwaway: insert a comma before it.

Whether or not to include a comma before an adverbial dependent clause is often a no-brainer.

 There's some Diet Pepsi in the refrigerator <u>if you're thirsty</u>.

This sentence implies, nonsensically, that if you're not thirsty, there isn't any soda in the refrigerator. The adverbial dependent clause *if you're thirsty* is a throwaway and needs to be punctuated as such, with a comma before it. The soda is in the refrigerator whether you are thirsty or not.

In the following specimen, the underlined adverbial dependent clause is also a throwaway and must be preceded by a comma.

 …the British painter Tom Fairs…did not begin producing art full time until after he retired from teaching at London's Central School of Art and Design (now Central Saint Martins) <u>when he was 60</u>. (*New York Times*)

In the following two excerpts, the underlined sentence-ending adverbial dependent clauses are must-haves.

 Last month, the F.T.C. informed Amazon that it planned to sue, <u>unless the company agreed to a consent order modeled after the Apple settlement</u>. (*New York Times*)

The comma after *sue* is lopping off a clausal limb vital to the meaning of the sentence. The comma must therefore be deleted.

 This may be why so many of us could relate to the NBC sitcom "The Office," with its universal message: The office would be a fine place to work, <u>if it weren't for everyone else</u>. (*Wall Street Journal*)

The comma before the adverbial dependent clause severs the clause from the body of the sentence, where it's needed to set a restriction on the meaning of the independent clause. The reader needs to understand that the office depicted in the sitcom would in fact not be a fine place to work. The comma after *work* must go away.

Sentences ending with adverbial dependent clauses that begin with *because* are especially vexatious. Chapter 74 discusses how to punctuate such sentences if the independent clause is phrased in the negative. Here, let's look at sentences in which the independent clause is phrased affirmatively.

Should the sentence *I decided to ask Joyelle instead of Jack because I needed an answer right away* include a comma before *because*? The answer is no if I want to emphasize the reason why I decided to ask one person instead of another. The answer is yes if I want to emphasize the decision itself and not the reason for it.

A writer, in short, must determine what she wants her sentence to emphasize, then punctuate the sentence accordingly. In some sentences, though, a writer has no choice.

Dogs everywhere are presumably barking, whimpering or growling with excitement, because the subscription service DogTV has just gone nationwide after a stretch of test marketing. (*New York Times*)

Readers need to know why the dogs are presumably so excited. The adverbial dependent clause is therefore a must-have, and the comma preceding it must vanish.

74 You don't want to omit the comma from this sentence, because the meaning will change.

Sentences that (1) begin with an independent clause including the adverb *not* in either full or contracted form and (2) end with an adverbial dependent clause starting with *because* (or with *since* or *as* used as a synonym for *because*) mean one thing if a comma separates the two clauses, and they mean something entirely different if there's no comma between the two clauses. Careful writers live with this fact the way they live with life's other complexities.

Consider this pair of sentences:

A: I don't want to go out tonight, because I feel hopeless.

B: I don't want to go out tonight because I feel hopeless.

The point of sentence A is *I don't want to go out tonight.*

Sentence B, however, means *I want to go out tonight—but for a reason other than the fact that I feel hopeless.*

Sentence A could end with the word *tonight,* and the meaning of the sentence would not change. All we would lose is the reason why I don't want to venture out tonight. That information, though, isn't essential to the sentence—and that's why the dependent clause in which it appears has been set off with a comma. The comma tells the reader that even though what comes next is something she doesn't really need, it is being given to her anyway. It's a throwaway.

But in sentence B, the information in the adverbial dependent clause is critical to the meaning of the sentence. The sentence can't do without it. It's setting a restriction on the meaning of the independent clause. So we can't cut the dependent clause loose with a comma. The dependent clause is a must-have.

Writers sometimes fail to recognize when a sentence-ending adverbial dependent clause beginning with *because* is a throwaway and thus fail to insert a comma before it. The result is a misinformative sentence.

 John McCain can't be bought by the special interests because he is guided by character, principle and a cause greater than himself—making a better America. (John McCain presidential-campaign mailing, 2008)

The campaign operative who wrote that sentence wasn't doing any favors for a senator running for president. The sentence literally means that McCain *can* be bought by special-interest groups—but for a reason other than the fact that he is guided by character, principle, and a cause greater than himself. The sentence needs a comma after *interests*.

75 Spurious Restrictives

A spurious restrictive is a word, a phrase, or a dependent clause forced against its will into distinguishing one thing or one person from another when the writer has intended to make no such distinction.

 While the band's 1968 debut *Vincebus Eruptum* set new standards for lumpen blues-rock brutality and was arguably the first heavy-metal album, Blue Cheer soon succumbed to a series of *Spinal Tap*-esque lineup changes and fell into obscurity.... (*The Rock Snob's Dictionary* [Broadway Books], by David Kamp and Steven Daly)

In the excerpt above, the writers wanted to cram as many details as possible into the fewest possible words. The writers' ambition to be hyperconcise is admirable, but the unhappy result is phrasing that, at the very least, puzzles or frustrates the reader and, at worst, misinforms her.

What did the writers intend to express?

 While the band's debut, *Vincebus Eruptum,* released in 1968, set new standards for lumpen blues-rock brutality....

That revision—which adds two words and three commas to the sentence—makes it immediately clear to the reader that Blue Cheer released only one debut album, that it happened to be called *Vincebus Eruptum,* and that it happened to be released in 1968. The album's title, *Vincebus Eruptum,* has been set off with commas because it is a throwaway appositive (see Chapter 66), providing information merely supplementary, not crucial, to the meaning of the sentence. The participial phrase *released in 1968* has also been set off with commas for a similar reason: the sentence could easily do without the phrase.

Any dutifully alert reader who attempted to decompress the information jammed into the subject slot of the introductory adverbial dependent clause of the phrasing in its original form, though, might have easily (and exasperatingly) been led to as many as three conclusions carrying her far from what the writers meant to say:

1. Blue Cheer's debut album that was released in 1968 is being differentiated from at least one other debut album that the band released in some other year. *1968* is functioning as a restrictive, must-have adjective—one that sets limits on the scope or range of meaning of the noun (*debut*) that follows it.

2. *Vincebus Eruptum* is being differentiated from at least one other debut album, with a different title, that Blue Cheer released. *Vincebus Eruptum* functions as a restrictive or must-have appositive (see Chapter 66), specifying one of Blue Cheer's debuts in particular.

Thus far, both the adjective preceding *debut* and the appositive following *debut* can readily be mistaken for restrictive elements. But there's still another possible misreading of the sentence.

3. The debut version of *Vincebus Eruptum* is being distinguished from another, later version of the same album, also recorded and released (under the same title) by Blue Cheer. In this interpretation, the noun *debut* is playing the role of a restrictive, must-have adjective.

The revision, then, with its responsibly positioned commas, spares the reader any of these hairsplitting agonies. A couple of commas and some minor rephrasing would do wonders for the following sentence as well.

 Hwang also wrote the book for the 2002 revival of "Flower Drum Song"; Kwan starred in the 1961 film version. (*New Yorker*)

Although there has been only one film version of the musical *Flower Drum Song*, the positioning of *1961* before *film version* implies that the 1961 film version is being differentiated from one or more other film versions. What makes the sentence even more misleading is the fact that as a staged musical, *Flower Drum Song* has been revived—on Broadway, that is—only once. *2002* is therefore another spurious restrictive.

 Hwang also wrote the book for the revival of "Flower Drum Song," in 2002; Kwan starred in the film version, in 1961.

 [from a review of the novel *We Had It So Good,* by Linda Grant] When Grant's fifth novel begins, Stephen Newman is a pampered child in postwar California. As it ends, he is a widower in contemporary London mourning his British wife. (*New Yorker*)

Because the second sentence informs readers that Newman is mourning his British wife (instead of, say, his Pennsylvania Dutch wife), anyone who recognizes the restrictive functioning of the adjective *British* can be forgiven for making the unintended inference that the fellow must have been married at least twice—an inference that conflicts with Newman's history in the novel. The sentence can be rephrased to prevent such misreading.

–89–

As it ends, he is a widower in contemporary London mourning his wife, who was British.

When you're presenting information about someone's parent, never insert a job title before the word *mother*, *mom*, *father*, or *dad*—unless you intend to imply that the person has had more than one mother or father.

 Her art-professor mom was a regular at Studio 54, and her dad is an ex-punk who used to frequent the same squat parties as Joe Strummer. (*Rolling Stone*)

Quick fix: Her mom, an art professor, was a regular. . . .

76 Quotations Serving as Objects and as Complements

Some writers feel an irresistible urge to insert a comma before every direct quotation. But there are only two kinds of sentences in which a comma before a quotation is correct. The first is a sentence in which a comma follows a verb of attribution: *Anna said, "I'm not sure I understand you."* The second is a sentence that includes a quotation serving as a throwaway appositive: *Her favorite expression, "No worries," got on her roommate's nerves.* That sort of sentence will require a pair of commas to set off the quotation, but if a quotation is positioned at the end of a sentence, there will be only one comma: *She stopped using her favorite expression, "No worries."* (Sentences in which quotations serve as appositives are discussed in Chapter 67.)

Direct quotations, however, also function the way ordinary single-word nouns function—as objects of prepositions, as direct objects of transitive verbs, as complements of linking verbs, and as object complements. And much as a writer would not insert a comma between a preposition and its object (nobody in her right mind would write *Anna loves bands like, Grizzly Bear*), a writer should not insert a comma between a preposition and a direct quotation serving as its object. The comma trailing the preposition *like* in the following sentence needs to vanish.

 Characters spout sentences like, "The plot thickens." (*New York Times*)

The commas preceding the direct quotations in the following sentences also need to take a powder.

 . . . servers protecting platters of pasta or empty glasses utter soft, "Pardon me's," hoping you will notice them. (*New York Times*) [The quotation is functioning as the direct object of the transitive verb *utter*. The comma following the quotation is needed to set off the sentence-ending participial phrase, a throwaway (see Chapter 71), but the quotation preceding that phrase must be repunctuated (*"Pardon me's,"*).]

 His philosophy is, "Make it easy for people to discover the content and know right away what it is." (*New York Times*) [The quotation is functioning as the complement of the linking verb *is*.]

–90–

Sometimes a direct quotation can serve even as the subject of a sentence. Do not insert a comma after the direct quotation. The following sentence needs to lose its comma.

 "I'm so goth I'm dead," is inscribed on a wall of a punk house in Minneapolis. (*New York Times*) [The subject of the sentence is *"I'm so goth I'm dead."*]

Lay off any commas following the participles *titled* and *entitled*. Such commas will always be wrong, as in the following sentence.

 At 17, I wrote a speech titled, "When You Come to the End of Your Days, Will You Be Able to Write Your Own Epitaph?" (*New York Times*)

77 Why compound the reader's frustration with a misreadable compound predicate?

Handbooks on grammar and punctuation routinely caution writers against inserting a comma before a coordinating conjunction (such as *and* or *but*) when it joins two halves of a compound predicate—that is, two verbs or verb phrases attached to a single subject, as in the sentence *She moved from Boston to rural Kansas and started a blog about her new life.* But a strict adherence to that rule is not always in a reader's best interest.

 [about the painter Eric Fischl] Adrift, he rejoined his family after they moved to Phoenix and enrolled in a community college art course "because no one fails art." (*Wall Street Journal*) [A hyphen should be inserted between *community* and *college*; see Chapter 86.]

In this complex sentence (a sentence consisting of one independent clause and one or more dependent clauses), it may take a millisecond or two for the reader to conclude with certainty that the subject of the verb phrase *enrolled in a community-college art course* is intended to be *he* (the subject of the independent clause), and not *they* (the subject of the adverbial dependent clause *after they moved to Phoenix*), despite the proximity of the pronoun *they* to the verb *enrolled*. But shouldn't a writer foresee a reader's potential trouble and take pains to prevent it? The sentence about Fischl is one in which a comma splitting the compound predicate is advisable to spare the reader any confusion.

 Adrift, he rejoined his family after they moved to Phoenix, and enrolled in a community-college art course "because no one fails art."

The comma after *Phoenix* forcibly divides the compound predicate into two halves; an alert reader is unlikely to attach *enrolled* to *they*.

Another option, of course, is to refashion the sentence as a compound-complex sentence (a sentence consisting of two independent clauses and one or more dependent clauses).

 Adrift, he rejoined his family after they moved to Phoenix, and he enrolled in a community-college art course "because no one fails art."

Punctuational Punctilio

78 Boundary Issues

Not knowing when or where one sentence comes to an end and the next one begins is no way for a writer to live. Yet the boundary between sentences—or, to be more precise, between independent clauses—often ends up mispunctuated. The result is the sentence-structure catastrophe classified as the comma-splice error.

 You can even listen without a computer, all you need is a network. (*New York Times*)

Teachers were once fond of the term *sentence sense,* which referred to a writer's intuitive grasp of whether a group of words is grammatically complete as a sentence. The term merits a revival, because sentence sense is on the decline. In the sample sentence, we should instantly recognize that the writer has in fact given us *two* sentences—*You can even listen without a computer* and *All you need is a network*—but hasn't erected a solid punctuational barrier between them. Each of those two sentences could stand on its own, so the writer might have simply replaced the comma with a period and uppercased the *a* in *all*.

 You can even listen without a computer. All you need is a network.

The writer most likely recognized, however, that the two sentences, or independent clauses, belonged together. The writer, that is, wanted a compound sentence—a sentence comprising two or more independent clauses closely related in meaning. The punctuation mark that the writer wanted was a semicolon, not a comma. A semicolon correctly separates two interrelated independent clauses.

 You can even listen without a computer; all you need is a network.

If the writer wanted to throw some dramatic emphasis on the second clause, the writer might have separated the clauses with a dash.

 You can even listen without a computer—all you need is a network.

The comma, though, was dead wrong. A comma can do a great many things, but one thing it can't do (except in one very special circumstance, discussed in the shaded box at the end of this chapter) is serve all alone as the divider between independent clauses.

Some mispunctuated compound sentences are crying out for a coordinating conjunction to follow the comma. (There are only seven coordinating conjunctions: *and, but, yet, or, nor, for,* and *so.*)

 All the smart kids are selling their old gadgets, why aren't you? (*New York Times*)

 All the smart kids are selling their old gadgets, so why aren't you selling yours?

Other mispunctuated compound sentences already include a different kind of conjunction—a conjunctive adverb—to join the two independent clauses, but the conjunctive adverb hasn't been punctuated correctly.

 Coat checkroom is complimentary, however we are not responsible for loss or damage. (sign inside the Four Seasons restaurant, visible in a *New York Times* photograph)

 By definition, American's [American Airlines'] customers are willing to pay for nonstop service, otherwise they would take US Airways' cheaper fare. (*Wall Street Journal*)

A semicolon, not a comma, must precede a conjunctive adverb that joins two independent clauses, and a comma must almost always follow the conjunctive adverb. There are far more conjunctive adverbs than there are coordinating conjunctions. The most frequently used conjunctive adverbs include *also, additionally, furthermore, finally, however, nevertheless, therefore, thus, consequently, indeed, similarly, likewise, meanwhile, soon, then, afterward,* and *later*. Transitional phrases such as the following often serve as conjunctive adverbs as well: *in addition, for example, for instance, in fact, after all, in other words, that is, that is to say, in conclusion, in short, to sum up, in sum,* and *in brief*.

The conjunctive adverb most frequently mispunctuated by professional writers is *then*, which happens to be one of the few conjunctive adverbs that don't require a comma afterward.

 Just getting the home page to open was hard, then it turned out that the instructions for choosing a username are defective. (*Wall Street Journal*)

The comma before *then* in that sentence could be replaced by a semicolon. An alternative is to insert the coordinating conjunction *and* after the comma preceding *then*.

Any writer who resorts to using *plus* as a conjunctive adverb must punctuate it as such.

 [The app] Tips for iPhone is intuitive and helpful, plus it's a great way to while away a few spare minutes. (*New York Times*)

Quick fix: substitute a semicolon for the comma, and insert a comma after *plus*.

A final type of comma-splice error occurs when a writer sandwiches attribution between halves of a direct quotation consisting of the equivalent of two complete sentences. A period or a semicolon, not a comma, must follow the attribution.

 "I was very fortunate to get there early," Mr. Black says of SoundCloud, which claims to have 20 million users, "I might have beat some of the larger radio stations to SoundCloud...." (*New York Times*)

"I was very fortunate to get there early," Mr. Black says of SoundCloud, which claims to have 20 million users. "I might have beat some of the larger radio stations to SoundCloud...."

PATTERNS FOR CORRECTLY PUNCTUATING COMPOUND SENTENCES

1. Independent clause + semicolon + independent clause + period

2. Independent clause + semicolon + conjunctive adverb + comma + independent clause + period

3. Independent clause + colon + independent clause + period (see Chapter 82)

4. Independent clause + dash + independent clause + period

5. Independent clause + opening parenthesis + independent clause + closing parenthesis + period (see Chapter 85)

Asyndeton is no sin.
A special kind of compound sentence requires nothing more than a comma between independent clauses. It's known as an asyndetonic compound sentence. *Asyndeton* simply means phrasing without conjunctions where a reader would ordinarily expect to find them. The classic example is Julius Caesar's *I came, I saw, I conquered*, but examples abound in contemporary writing.

The Caesar quotation illustrates the two most striking characteristics of an asyndetonic sentence: the independent clauses must be brief, and they must be grammatically parallel (see Chapter 41).

There are two varieties of asyndetonic sentences. The first, to which the Caesar quotation belongs, consists of compound sentences in which there are two or more independent clauses expressing an additive relationship: the coordinating conjunction *and* is implied between the second-last and final clauses: *We tried, we failed, we tried again*. The second category consists of variations on the *It's not X, it's Y* pattern, which is often called contrastive or antithetical phrasing: *It's not the heat, it's the humidity*.

Asyndetonic phrasing can be stylish and sophisticated, but it's best used sparingly.

79 At the time I was writing sentences that could be mistaken for fragments.

Readers of that title will fall into two groups. The first will consist of readers generous enough in spirit to recognize that the writer simply forgot to insert a much-needed comma after *time*. They will good-naturedly insert a mental comma and go on with their lives.

The second group, though, will be thinking, Where's the other half of the sentence? They will have intuited that the phrase *at the time* is functioning similarly to a subordinating conjunction such as *when* or *while*. In short, they will misread the word-group as a fragment, because they've been led to expect the arrival of an independent clause—such as *I was getting lots of dirty looks*—to explain what else was happening at that same time and thereby to complete the sentence. Such readers will feel no frustration, though, if they see a comma after *time*.

Easily misreadable sentences beginning with *at the time* or *at the same time* are common. In the following sentence, a comma after *time* will set things right.

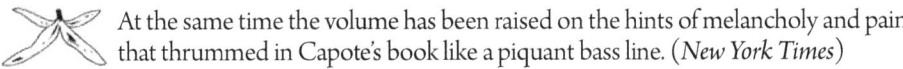
At the same time the volume has been raised on the hints of melancholy and pain that thrummed in Capote's book like a piquant bass line. (*New York Times*)

Sentences readily misinterpretable as fragments almost always begin with an unpunctuated introductory adverbial phrase—sometimes prepositional (as in the examples above), sometimes not. A comma after the adverbial phrase *While in junior high school* at the start of the following sentence will save the day.

While in junior high school he moved with his parents to Houston, where he worked after school each day in the cafe opened by his father. (*New York Times*)

80 An interruptive element in a sentence—don't forget has to be set off with punctuation at both ends.

Asymmetrical punctuation, such as that in the title of this chapter (which needs another dash after *forget*), is too common for us to write it off as merely a typographical error. Maybe it's a punctuational symptom of our culture of acceleration, in which we're so rushed that we sometimes end up doing things by halves.

An interruptive element—a word, a phrase, or a dependent clause with which a writer delivers supplemental information to a reader—needs punctuation both before and after it. A pair of commas, parentheses, or dashes will do the trick. Of the two interruptive elements (*a new documentary film* and *though politely*) in the following excerpt, only the second has been correctly punctuated at both ends.

"Salinger," a new documentary film touches—though politely—on the story. . . . (*New York Times*)

Asymmetrical punctuation often afflicts sentences in which the interruptive element includes parenthesized phrasing at its end. A comma must follow the closing parenthesis in the following sentence.

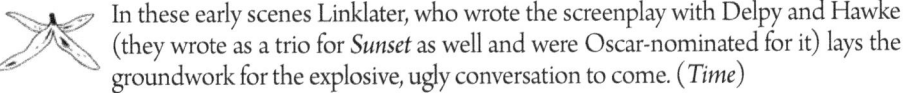
In these early scenes Linklater, who wrote the screenplay with Delpy and Hawke (they wrote as a trio for *Sunset* as well and were Oscar-nominated for it) lays the groundwork for the explosive, ugly conversation to come. (*Time*)

81 Semicolonic Blockages

Every semicolon erects a much-needed barrier between major structural components of a sentence. Sometimes, unfortunately, the barriers are set up in places that make for rough going in the sentence's verbal pathway. The semicolons become obstructions. A writer's use of semicolons should never obscure the design of a sentence—particularly the jointure where the subject meets the predicate. In fact, the only phrasing a reader should ever expect to find after a semicolon is either (1) the equivalent of another complete sentence or (2) one or more additional elements in a series (a) that will bring a sentence to a close or (b) that is set off, with dashes or parentheses, as an interruptive element.

One of the standard uses of the semicolon is to separate items in a series when at least one of them includes a comma as interior punctuation.

 Other liaisons included one with Simon Youngman, a diamond heir, Alexander Spencer-Churchill, the scion of several posh houses, and her latest, Alex Loudon, 30, a cricketer and financier. (*New York*)

 Other liaisons have included one with Simon Youngman, a diamond heir; Alexander Spencer-Churchill, the scion of several posh houses; and, her latest, Alex Loudon, 30, a cricketer and financier.

In that sentence, the series (functioning as the direct object of the transitive verb *included*) brings the sentence to an end. When a reader sees a semicolon, she expects it to be followed by phrasing equivalent in grammatical status to the phrasing that precedes it. Her expectations will not be thwarted as long as a series in which semicolons separate the items is positioned at the end of a sentence. Increasingly, though, writers are positioning a semicoloned series at the very start of a sentence or, without strong enough punctuation to set it off, somewhere in the middle of a sentence—and the results can be disorienting.

 Most important, [Roy] Lichtenstein's large-featured images, with their Ben-Day dot patterns; thick, black contours; and flat, bright colors are almost ergonomically comfortable to the eye. (*New York Times*)

A reader can't help sensing that things are seriously out of whack in the design of that sentence. The punctuational dividers between the elements in the midsentence series are stronger than the one between the two principal parts of the sentence: the complete subject (*Lichtenstein's large-featured images*) and the predicate (*are almost ergonomically comfortable to the eye*), both of which flap about flimsily at the beginning and the end instead of striking a reader as weighted and stationary. The semicolons become punctuational blockades and wall off the three parts of the series from each other so solidly that the dividing line between the simple subject and the first word of the predicate (that is, between *images* and *are*)—which should be the most conspicuous line of demarcation in the sentence—ends up obscured, because the writer failed to insert a comma after *colors* to mark the end of the long interruptive element. In fact, it's easy for a reader to misconstrue *and flat, bright colors are almost ergonomically comfortable to the eye* as an independent clause unto itself, a misreading that would lead the reader to believe that the three items in the series are nonparallel (see Chapter 41).

The result is an ungainly sentence; it looks off-kilter. Most of the weight of the sentence is in the long prepositional phrase attached to the subject. In the revision below, the core words of the subject and of the predicate (*images* and *are*, respectively) stand out unmistakably.

 Most important, Lichtenstein's large-featured images—with their Benday-dot patterns; thick, black contours; and flat, bright colors—are almost ergonomically comfortable to the eye. OR: Substitute parentheses for the dashes.

When the introductory phrasing of a sentence includes a series whose elements are set off by semicolons, substitute commas for the semicolons and parenthesize any supplementary phrasing, or rework the introductory element so that semicolons are no longer needed.

 From a pair of seven-foot-tall Sukuma guardian figures, staring gravely down at whoever approaches; to a five-inch-long Chagga ceramic female form nestled, like an infant, in a banana-leaf cradle; to a row of beaded Tabwa masks from the museum's permanent collection, this is a sensational array. (*New York Times*)

 From a pair of seven-foot-tall Sukuma guardian figures (staring gravely down at whoever approaches), to a five-inch-long Chagga ceramic female form (nestled, like an infant, in a banana-leaf cradle), to a row of beaded Tabwa masks from the museum's permanent collection, this is a sensational array.

Or you might simply turn such a sentence on its head to eliminate the top-heaviness.

 This sensational array of treasures ranges from a pair of seven-foot-tall Sukuma guardian figures, staring gravely down at whoever approaches; to a five-inch-long Chagga ceramic female form nestled, like an infant, in a banana-leaf cradle; to a row of beaded Tabwa masks from the museum's permanent collection.

When a series whose elements are set off with semicolons functions as the subject of a sentence, rewrite the sentence so that semicolons are no longer needed in the subject, or use an inverted-sentence pattern.

 Reddit, a community discussion site; Boing Boing, the culture blog; and the comedy video site My Damn Channel were blacked out. (*New York Times*)

 The community-discussion site Reddit, the culture blog Boing Boing, and the comedy-video site My Damn Channel were blacked out. OR: Among the blacked-out sites were Reddit, a community-discussion site; Boing Boing, a culture blog; and My Damn Channel, a comedy-video site.

82 Irritating Colons

A reader expects that a colon following an independent clause will serve as a gateway to phrasing that offers examples or elaborations or clarifications to supplement and enrich her understanding of what has already been stated. The colon is a portal to climactic phrasing that will wrap things up for a sentence. A reader encountering a colon therefore has every reason to believe that a terminal punctuation mark is just around the corner. The last thing she expects is that after presenting the examples or elaborations or clarifications, the sentence will get its second wind and go heading off in a new direction. But writers sometimes forget that a colon signals that sentential closure is about to be achieved.

 Mr. Johnson liked to tell employees that there were two kinds of people: believers and skeptics, and at Apple, there were only believers. (*New York Times*)

The reader of the phrasing that precedes the colon in that sentence will be correct in assuming that the only business remaining to be done is to specify the two types of people into which all of humankind is divisible. Because the writer has positioned a colon after *people*, the sentence has to come to an end after *believers and skeptics*. Its work will then be finished. Instead, though, the writer keeps moving forward after the specification and delivers a second statement. And by annexing an independent clause (the equivalent of a stand-alone sentence) to the noun phrase following the colon, the writer has failed to respect and honor boundaries. The results are ramshackle. A writer gets one shot at winding things up after a colon—and that's it. In the phrasing that follows a colon, there can be no second acts.

Mr. Johnson liked to tell employees that there were two kinds of people: believers and skeptics. And at Apple, he would go on to say, there were only believers. OR [the writer is free to dispose of the colon]: Mr. Johnson liked to tell employees that there were two kinds of people—believers and skeptics—and that at Apple there were only believers.

It's perhaps unfair to consider the epigraph a microcosm of the book as a whole, or to believe we hear the author's voice in the borrowed words she's chosen to introduce her story, but readers do. Thus when I happened on M. F. K. Fisher's "The Gastronomical Me" (1943) in a secondhand book store and read the epigraph: "To be happy you must have taken the measure of your powers, tasted the fruit of your passion and learned your place in the world (Santayana)," I knew I had met an author who would be a lifelong companion and guide. (*Wall Street Journal*)

Here, in the second sentence of the excerpt, the colon introducing the quotation leads the reader to assume that the sentence will call it quits as soon as Santayana has had his say. The trouble, though, is not only that the quotation is followed by the equivalent of a complete sentence but also that the phrasing preceding the colon is merely an adverbial dependent clause. Any colon introducing a quotation needs to be preceded either by a word-group consisting of at least an independent clause (even something as short and sweet as *She said*) or by a simple little word or phrase such as *Thus* or *Another example*.

In the mispunctuated sentence above, the quotation is functioning as a throwaway appositive (see Chapter 67). The quotation thus needs to be set off at both ends with symmetrical punctuation—a pair of commas (not a stylistically desirable alternative here, though, because the quotation already includes a comma within its phrasing), a pair of dashes, or a pair of parentheses—and not with the asymmetrical punctuation of a colon at one end and a comma at the other (see Chapter 80).

Thus, when I happened on M. F. K. Fisher's "The Gastronomical Me" (1943) in a secondhand-book store and read the epigraph, from Santayana—"To be happy you must have taken the measure of your powers, tasted the fruit of your passion, and learned your place in the world"—I knew I had met an author who would be a lifelong companion and guide. OR [to eliminate a multitasking dash (see Chapter 84)]: Thus, when I happened on M. F. K. Fisher's "The Gastronomical Me" (1943) in a secondhand-book store and read the epigraph, from Santayana ("To be happy you must have taken the measure of your powers, tasted the fruit of your passion, and learned your place in the world"), I knew I had met an author who would be a lifelong companion and guide.

83 The overdashed sentence is not a dashing one.

Although it might seem dictatorial to issue a decree limiting the number of times a punctuation mark might legitimately appear in a single sentence, you will be doing your readers a favor if you restrict yourself to no more than two dashes in any sentence. One would never make such a restriction on parentheses, however, even though a pair of dashes and a pair of parentheses share a common function: to set off interruptive elements. But among the ways in which paired dashes and paired parentheses differ is in their very appearance. An opening parenthesis is immediately identifiable by its shape; the same goes for a closing parenthesis. An opening dash and a closing dash, though, are indistinguishable.

In a sentence with a slew of parentheses, a reader will never be confused about where an interruptive element begins and where it ends. A sentence with a design such as the following presents no problems for a reader.

_____(_____)_____(_____)_____
(_____)_____(_____).

Without even reading words, a reader can tell not only that there are four interruptive elements but also where each one starts and finishes.

But what about a sentence like the following?

_____—_____—_____—_____—_____
—_____—_____—_____.

Before reaching the midpoint, many readers will be pitched into uncertainty about whether any particular dash marks the beginning or the end of an interruptive element.

Bear in mind, as well, that a closing parenthesis is often followed by another punctuation mark (most frequently a comma, but sometimes a semicolon, a colon, or even a dash). Those additional punctuation marks further help the reader to take in the overall design of a sentence.

_____(_____),_____(_____),_____
(_____);_____(_____).

A dash, on the other hand (see Chapter 84), is never followed by another punctuation mark within a sentence.

When you find yourself using more than one pair of dashes in a sentence, ask yourself whether all but one of the dashed-off elements might be enclosed between parentheses (or set off with commas) instead. It's best to reserve the dashes for the interruptive element of greatest importance. In the second sentence in the excerpt below, neither dashed-off element seems more important than the other, so substituting parentheses for dashes is fine for both elements. Some confusion arises, though, about whether the writer intended the second interruptive element to end with *rip* or with *Cline*—and this confusion is a further example of why parentheses are more reader-friendly than dashes in such a sentence.

 Angel Olsen sang 10 songs at the Glasslands Gallery on Monday night. . . . She beamed forth with a voice that switched between lax—quiet, neutral, relaxed—and over the top—semi-operatic, jumping notes in a warbling rip, in a few 50-year-old ways pointing toward English folk music and Patsy Cline. (*New York Times*)

 She beamed forth with a voice that switched between lax (quiet, neutral, relaxed) and over the top (semioperatic, jumping notes in a warbling rip), in a few 50-year-old ways pointing toward English folk music and Patsy Cline. OR: She beamed forth with a voice that switched between lax (quiet, neutral, relaxed) and over the top (semioperatic, jumping notes in a warbling rip, in a few 50-year-old ways pointing toward English folk music and Patsy Cline).

In some sentences with two pairs of dashes, however, a reader cannot always be confident that the writer intended to place equal emphasis on both dashed-off elements. It's to the reader's advantage, then, for a writer to save the dashes for setting off the interruptive element of greater importance.

 This spring, it has been disturbing to see a number of college commencement speakers withdraw—or have their invitations rescinded—after protests from students and—to me, shockingly—from senior faculty and administrators who should know better. (Michael Bloomberg, in his commencement address at Harvard University, in 2014, quoted in *Wall Street Journal*)

 [emphasizing Bloomberg's shocked response] This spring, it has been disturbing to see a number of college-commencement speakers withdraw, or have their invitations rescinded, after protests from students and—to me, shockingly—from senior faculty and administrators, who should know better.

 [emphasizing the rescinded invitations] This spring, it has been disturbing to see a number of college-commencement speakers withdraw—or have their invitations rescinded—after protests from students and, shockingly to me, from senior faculty and administrators, who should know better.

Overdashed sentences can cause other mischief, too.

 Women adored Otto's lips—modeled and sensual, like a young Richard Burton's—his darkly tanned skin, his sexy habit of speaking through a haze of cigarette smoke, one eye half-closed—and the fact that, as his later cohort Theodore Draper said, "above all, he could not be accused of dullness." (*The Girls: Sappho Goes to Hollywood* [St. Martin's Press], by Diane McLellan)

A sentence like the one above can leave a reader vertiginous. The trouble is the ease with which she can mistake the second and third dashes for enclosive dashes, as well as the ease with which she can lose her grasp of whether there are two consecutive interruptive phrases instead of just one. Making matters worse, the second dash is a multitasking dash (see Chapter 84). The eccentric and unhelpful punctuation of the sentence obscures the uncomplicated structure, in which a transitive verb (*adored*) is followed by a series of four direct objects.

Women adored Otto's lips, modeled and sensual, like a young Richard Burton's; his darkly tanned skin; his sexy habit of speaking through a haze of cigarette smoke, one eye half-closed; and the fact that, as his later cohort Theodore Draper said, "above all, he could not be accused of dullness."

84 The Multitasking Dash

Something seems more than slightly off—to exacting readers, anyway—when the closing dash in a pair of dashes has been asked to function simultaneously in two different ways: (1) as the second half of a pair of dashes setting set off interruptive phrasing and (2) as the equivalent of a comma (or a semicolon, or even a single dash—that is, a dash that is not half of a pair).

A dash works best when it's asked to perform only one function. A multitasking dash easily dumbfounds a reader.

 The air around them is charged with anxiety—about the threat of nuclear war, mostly—intellectual restlessness and sexual curiosity. (*New York Times*)

The second dash is the source of the confusion. A reader needs a few seconds to discern the architecture of the phrasing and conclude that the sentence is presenting a three-element series and that the first element is followed by a pair of interruptive prepositional phrases. The second dash is being asked (1) to bring an interruptive element to its close, which, of course, a dash is perfectly capable of doing (much as a closing parenthesis or a comma would be), and (2) to separate the second item in a series from the first, which only a comma (or a semicolon [see Chapter 81]) can do. The poor reader is expected to recognize that the dash has been called upon to perform two entirely different roles.

Ideally, when a dashed-off element is removed from a sentence, what remains should be perfectly intelligible, as in the following example.

 Her best qualities—empathy, social intelligence, a willingness to collaborate—account for her success as a manager.

Extract the dashed-off interruptive element from the *Times* sentence under consideration above, though, and you're left with the unpunctuated near-nonsense of *The air around them is charged with anxiety intellectual restlessness and sexual curiosity*. The words *anxiety* and *intellectual* abut in a meaning-defeating way.

In sentences of that sort, the reader is better served by parentheses, because a comma can follow a closing parenthesis but cannot (in post-nineteenth-century punctuation) follow a dash. Filling the slot between *anxiety* and *intellectual restlessness* is going to require the insertion of more than one kind of punctuation mark.

 The air around them is charged with anxiety (about the threat of nuclear war, mostly), intellectual restlessness, and sexual curiosity.

 But it tastes like magic: smooth, sweet, and spicy—depending on a changing roster of seasonings, such as bergamot tea and Thai bird chili—topped off with your choice of spirit and served over a gigantic ice cube. (*New Yorker*)

Delete the dashed-off phrasing, and *spicy* crashes unpunctuatedly into *topped*: *But it tastes like magic: smooth, sweet, and spicy topped off with your choice of spirit....*

 But it tastes like magic: smooth, sweet, and spicy (depending on a changing roster of seasonings, such as bergamot tea and Thai bird chili), topped off with your choice of spirit....

A rule, then? If the removal of any dashed-off phrasing results in the abutment of two grammatically or syntactically incompatible words, replace the pair of dashes with a pair of parentheses, and insert after the closing parenthesis whichever punctuation mark, such as a comma, is needed to ensure smooth, effortless reading.

A sentence with a multitasking dash can sometimes leave a reader confused about which noun or nouns constitute the subject.

 So the characters' bearing, as much as their more pronounced actions—and their words—creates the drama. (*New Yorker*)

Short as the sentence is, it invites misunderstanding. Sensing that the first dash might be functioning as a comma as well, a reader may initially be tempted to attach the dashed-off phrasing *and their words* to *bearing* (and thereby construe *as much as their more pronounced actions* as an interruptive element); but then, jolted by the dissonance between what has seemed to be an additive-compound subject (*bearing* and *words*) and the singular verb (*creates*), she will realize that she has misread the sentence: the subject is *bearing,* and the interruptive element is *and their words.*

 So the characters' bearing, as much as their more pronounced actions (and their words), creates the drama. OR: So the characters' bearing—as much as their more pronounced actions and their words—creates the drama.

85 Punctuating Parentheses

Parentheses signal to a reader that the phrasing they enclose is of secondary importance to a sentence. The only trouble they cause a writer is the trouble of determining whether a punctuation mark should be inserted inside or outside the closing parenthesis. The rules, though, are uncomplicated.

If an entire freestanding sentence is parenthesized between two other freestanding sentences (or at the end of a paragraph), the terminal punctuation mark of the parenthesized sentence is positioned inside, not outside, the closing parenthesis.

 As [Richard] Hell notes, The Voidoids' subversive aim was to strike a balance between intellectual complexity and jagged punk, a tricky approach perfected in the band's 1977 debut, *Blank Generation*. (In *Clean Tramp*, Hell says he prefers the band's decent but shaky 1982 follow-up, *Destiny Street*, for reasons as perverse as many he maintains throughout the book). His writing is equally eccentric and erratic. (*The Onion*'s *A.V. Club*)

The parenthesized sentence must end like this: *book.*)

When a parenthesized sentence-within-a-sentence is positioned at the end of a hosting sentence, the period follows the closing parenthesis.

 [Jorie] Graham doesn't lack a sense of the tragic; but the tragic is treated the same as the injured dog (she has a moral imagination both icy and sentimental.) (*New Criterion*)

The sentence must end like this: *sentimental*).

There are three other matters to bear in mind about parenthesizing entire sentences within hosting sentences: (1) the phrasing of a parenthesized sentence-within-a-sentence must never end with any punctuation mark unless the parenthesized sentence-within-a-sentence ends with an abbreviation (such as *p.m.*) that requires a period at its end or unless the parenthesized sentence is interrogative or exclamatory, in which case it requires a question mark or an exclamation point at its end; (2) the first word of the parenthesized sentence-within-a-sentence is capitalized only if it is a word that always requires capitalization; and (3) when a writer parenthesizes two consecutive sentences within a hosting sentence, the result is often unsightly, and the matter of when and when not to capitalize becomes a little more complicated, as the following sentence illustrates.

 Her daughter has had an unusual work history (she struggled for two years as a freelance writer. Then she was hired as a publicist for a film-production company), but her son has been unemployed since the recession.

Notice that in the parenthesized element, only the second of the two-in-a-row parenthesized sentences begins with an uppercased letter. Notice, too, that only the first of the two parenthesized sentences ends with a period.

Four final guidelines about curvy punctuation:

First, most parenthesized elements are not the equivalent of complete sentences.

 When her husband lost his job (an unexpected turn of events), he became a stay-at-home father.

A comma follows the closing parenthesis in that sentence, because if the parenthetical phrasing were omitted, a comma would need to follow *job*. But when the parenthesized element is added to the sentence right after *job*, the adverbial dependent clause (*When her husband lost his job*) and the parenthesized element now form a single, solid unit—and the comma must be positioned at its end. Even if the parenthesized element is the equivalent of a complete sentence, as in *When her husband lost his job (this was an unexpected turn of events), he became a stay-at-home father,* the comma still follows the closing parenthesis.

Second, if a parenthesized element of any sort (a single word, a phrase, a dependent clause, or, as discussed earlier, an independent clause) has been included at the end of the hosting sentence, the period (or other terminal punctuation mark) must be positioned after the closing parenthesis.

 Rodarte parlays mohair into a dress so loosely knit as to be virtually see-through (and with matching briefs.) (*New York Times*)

The sentence must end like this: *briefs*).

Third, as with a parenthesized sentence-within-a-sentence, any other parenthesized phrasing must begin with a lowercased word unless the first word is a word always requiring capitalization.

 ...this was a fine Armani display of realism and beauty (Gosh, a pantsuit unaccompanied by a funny hat!) that was overdue. (*New York Times*)

The parenthesized element must begin like this: (*gosh*,

Finally, forget about inserting any punctuation mark before an opening parenthesis.

 ...Crosby Braverman, the California man-child Mr. Shepard plays on "Parenthood," (53 episodes and counting), is so indelible that, like it or not, everything else Mr. Shepard does registers as a pallid reflection. (*New York Times*)

The comma after the *d* in "*Parenthood*" must disappear.

86 Why not learn the use-hyphens-between-words-that-together-form-an-adjectival-compound-preceding-a-noun rule?

That intentionally inelegant title reminds us of a widely neglected use of the hyphen, the least understood of all the punctuation marks. We often write sentences in which two or more words team up to form a phrase that functions like a single-word adjective. In the sentence *An eight-year-old girl lives across the street,* for instance, the phrase *eight-year-old* serves much the same way as the adjective *young* does in the sentence *A young girl lives across the street.* Whenever such a phrase precedes a noun, the writer needs to stitch its words together with hyphens so that a reader instantly recognizes that the words constitute a single unit. It's best, though, for a writer to keep her adjectival compounds fairly short—between, say, two words and five.

Following are thirteen rudiments of reader-friendly hyphenation. In the excerpts, the adjectival compounds requiring hyphenation (or, in rule 7, not requiring hyphenation) are boldfaced.

1. A **NOUN+NOUN** combination serving as an adjective and preceding a noun requires a hyphen.

 ...often trivialized as a **beauty pageant** fluff bunny, she has an underlying rigor and poise and mainstream appeal.... (*Attack Poodles and Other Media Mutants: The Looting of the News in a Time of Terror* [Miramax Books], by James Wolcott)

Quick fix: a beauty-pageant fluff bunny [Note that *fluff bunny,* like *teddy bear,* is a compound noun.]

This first rule also applies to a **NOUN+GERUND** combination preceding a noun.

 I made my first big catch as a foundry proofreader in one of the **Christmas shopping** columns. (*Between You & Me: Confessions of a Comma Queen* [Norton, first edition], by Mary Norris)

Quick fix: Christmas-shopping columns

2. An **ADJECTIVE+NOUN** combination serving as an adjective and preceding a noun requires a hyphen.

 A **rare book** sale at Doyle (April 15) includes a pile of love letters.... (*New Yorker*)

Quick fix: A rare-book sale

This second rule also applies to an **ADJECTIVE+GERUND** combination preceding a noun.

 How about a **competitive eating** champion? (*Beautiful & Pointless: A Guide to Modern Poetry* [Harper], by David Orr)

Quick fix: a competitive-eating champion

3. A **NOUN+ADJECTIVE** combination serving as an adjective and preceding a noun requires a hyphen.

 I am not thinking of **child protective** services.... (*New Yorker*)

Quick fix: child-protective services

4. A **NOUN+PARTICIPLE** combination serving as an adjective and preceding a noun requires a hyphen.

 ...Giambattista Valli offered white **flower embroidered** shifts and mini coats. (*New York Times*)

Quick fix: flower-embroidered shifts

5. A **PARTICIPLE+NOUN** combination serving as an adjective and preceding a noun requires a hyphen.

 He taught in the **continuing education** program.... (*New Yorker*'s Page-Turner blog)

Quick fix: the continuing-education program

6. Always insert a hyphen between the adverb *well* and a participle when the two words precede a noun.

 ...the company had "appropriately extended these **well researched** play patterns into the digital space." (*New York Times*)

Quick fix: well-researched play patterns

7. Do not insert a hyphen between an adverb ending in *ly* and an adjective or a participle when the two words precede a noun.

 The wonderful reporters and writers I met in the **dimly-lighted** corridors were now my *colleagues*. (*Here but Not Here: My Life with William Shawn and* The New Yorker [Random House], by Lillian Ross)

Quick fix: the dimly lighted corridors

8. Always insert a hyphen between an adverb not ending in *ly* and a participle when the two words precede a noun.

 ... he got stuck in **slow moving** traffic near Mahim. (*Bollywood Life*)

Quick fix: slow-moving traffic

9. Often an adjectival-compound phrase modifying a noun consists of more than two words and therefore requires more than one hyphen.

 "Another **desert island cartoon** clipping from my uncle." (cartoon caption, *New Yorker*)

Quick fix: "Another desert-island-cartoon clipping from my uncle."

 ... I waited for the street cleaner to go by, in the street ballet called **alternate side of the street** parking.... (*Between You & Me: Confessions of a Comma Queen* [Norton, first edition], by Mary Norris)

Quick fix: the street ballet called alternate-side-of-the-street parking

10. A spelled-out multiword number is hyphen-free when it functions as an adjective preceding a noun (*two hundred and thirty hours*) or when it functions as a complement (*The total is now exactly seven hundred and twenty*) unless such a number includes a fraction, which requires a hyphen (*We sat through six and one-third innings*), or unless the number is one that always requires a hyphen (*two hundred and thirty-three hours*). But a spelled-out multiword number must be hyphenated when it unites with a noun to form an adjectival compound modifying another noun (*a two-hour-and-fifteen-minute movie*).

 The children's spring collection from Nina stars a ... sandal with a one-**and** a-half-inch wood heel ($48.95). (*New York Times*)

Quick fix: a one-and-a-half-inch wood heel

11. Use suspensive hyphens when two or more adjectival compounds preceding a noun have a second word in common—such as the word *grade* in the phrase *first-, second-, and third-grade students.* Suspensive hyphens enable you to avoid the unnecessary repetition of the second word. Either a comma or a blank space must follow each suspensive hyphen.

 ...younger Nigerians from **middle** and **upper class** families are more eager to have and be seen with the latest gadget or accessory. (*Wall Street Journal*)

Quick fix: middle- and upper-class families

12. Insert hyphens when you're presenting measurements in phrasing that calls for the preposition *by*: *Print out your final draft on 8½-by-11-inch paper.* (There is no blank space before or after the hyphens.)

13. Insert hyphens in inclusive phrasing that uses the preposition *to*: *She has a nine-to-five job. The program is aimed at an 8-to-27-year-old audience.* These sorts of hyphens, which are used to indicate a range or a span (of time, of ages, etc.), are often confused with suspensive hyphens. Suspensive hyphens, however, appear in phrasing that includes the conjunction *and* (or occasionally *or*, as in *five- or six-year-old students*). (An obvious but rare exception is the suspensive hyphen in phrasing such as *the mid- to late 1960s.*) The sentence *Eight- and eighteen-year-old students have completely different preoccupations* concerns only two groups of students: those who are eight years old and those who are eighteen. The sentence *The program appeals to eight-to-eighteen-year-old viewers*, in contrast, encompasses all viewers between the ages of eight and eighteen (including nine-year-olds, ten-year-olds, etc.). There is no space before or after hyphens in inclusive phrasing.

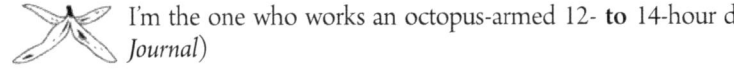 I'm the one who works an octopus-armed 12- **to** 14-hour day.... (*Wall Street Journal*)

Quick fix: an octopus-armed 12-to-14-hour day

This chapter has concerned itself with adjectival compounds, but writers also need to include all of the necessary hyphens in compound nouns that express a range or a span.

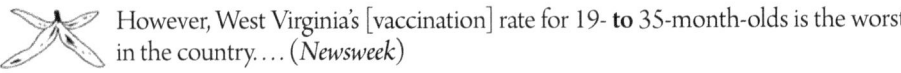 However, West Virginia's [vaccination] rate for 19- **to** 35-month-olds is the worst in the country.... (*Newsweek*)

Quick fix: 19-to-35-month-olds

Suspensive hyphens are needed in pairs or series of compound nouns that share one or more words at their end.

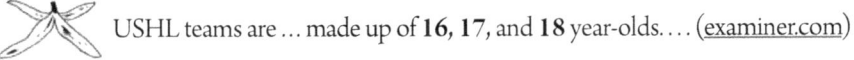 USHL teams are ... made up of **16, 17,** and **18** year-olds.... (examiner.com)

Quick fix: 16-, 17-, and 18-year-olds

87 We need more precise explanations.

What does the title of this chapter mean? We already have some precise explanations but need more? Or we need explanations that are more precise than the ones we already have?

If the writer means the latter, she would be doing readers a favor by uniting the adverb *more* and the adjective *precise* with a hyphen to form an adjectival compound: *We need more-precise explanations.* (Or she could rephrase the sentence: *We need explanations that are more precise.*)

The rules are simple enough. Hyphenate the combination of *more* and an adjective or a participle when you're making a qualitative statement (*She asked for more-persuasive evidence*). Leave the combination unhyphenated when you're making a quantitative statement (*She asked for more persuasive evidence*).

Readers sometimes find themselves initially puzzled about whether *more* is intended to imply quantity or quality.

 [about the books *J. D. Salinger: The Escape Artist*, by Thomas Beller, and *My Salinger Year*, by Joanna Rakoff] A year after the release of Shane Salerno and David Shields's scandalous biography [of J. D. Salinger] (along with a much-derided companion docudrama), two more personal and sympathetic takes prove worthy (if minor) correctives. (*New York*'s vulture.com)

The writer's sentence inadvertently (and self-contradictingly) states that in addition to the personal and sympathetic works about Salinger produced by Salerno and Shields, two more such works, by other writers, have now arrived. What the writer really means, though, is that the books by Beller and Rakoff are more personal and more sympathetic than the book and the film by Salerno and Shields. *More*, in this instance, is intended to emphasize quality, not quantity.

 …two more-personal and more-sympathetic takes prove worthy (if minor) correctives. OR: …two new takes, more personal and more sympathetic, prove worthy (if minor) correctives.

The combination of *less* and an adjective should not be hyphenated.

 It found that 54 percent of reports contained less-serious errors. (*San Francisco Chronicle*)

Such a sentence will not cause confusion about the distinction between the qualitative and the quantitative if both the writer and the reader understand that only the adjective *fewer*, and not *less*, can correctly be used to emphasize countable units (see Chapter 95).

88 This is no way to get from here-there.

There is no way you would ever write a sentence like that, instead of *This is no way to get from here to there*. So it's time to stop writing sentences like the following.

 Richie Ramone, 56, was the Ramones' drummer from 1982-87. (*Wall Street Journal*)

Phrasing that specifies a span of time is not exempt from the requirement that the preposition *from* be balanced with the preposition *to* in any sort of phrasing about a span or range or crossover from one thing or person to another.

Often, however, you can easily rewrite such sentences by discarding the preposition *from* and retaining the hyphen. (In the publishing world, an en dash would be used.)

 Graph shows figures from June-November 2001. (*New York Times*)

Quick fix: Graph shows June-November 2001 figures.

Similarly, much as you would never write *This is between you-me,* you can't get away with a sentence like this:

 Between 1996-2005, for example, the Treasury Department estimates that about half of the taxpayers in the bottom 20% moved into a higher income bracket. (*Wall Street Journal*)

Quick fix: Between 1996 and 2005, for example. . . .

89 Any friend of Erin's is a friend of mine.

One of the many peculiarities of the English language is a construction that grammarians refer to as the double possessive (or, more formally, the double genitive). We are apt to write *a colleague of Sara's,* rather than *a colleague of Sara,* but we sometimes can't help feeling a little funny about tacking on that apostrophe and the *s*. The prepositional phrase *of Sara,* after all, already seems to be doing the possessive-marking work. The double possessive, though, is both idiomatic and perfectly correct. We would never write *No dog of Andrea is ever going to sleep outside* instead of *No dog of Andrea's is ever going to sleep outside.* (Nor would we ever write *a neighbor of her* instead of *a neighbor of hers.*)

Complicating matters is the fact that, for nouns, the presence or the absence of the apostrophe and the *s* sometimes makes a big difference in meaning. It's clear from the phrase *a criticism of Heather* that Heather is the object of criticism; the phrase *a criticism of Heather's,* however, situates Heather as the person expressing the criticism. (The same is true of the distinction between *a criticism of her* and *a criticism of hers.*)

Aside from instances in which the intended meaning dictates that the possessive form of the noun or pronoun not be used, though, a writer mindful of grammar ought to accept the double possessive as one of the cherishable eccentricities of our language. The following sentence would therefore benefit from an apostrophe and an *s* after *mother.*

 She and her two younger brothers bounced around foster homes for two years, before a friend of her mother took them to live with their paternal grandmother in Havana. (*New York Times*) [The comma should be deleted; see Chapter 73.]

90 The Propriety of Punctuational Threesomes

We're accustomed to seeing two consecutive punctuation marks whenever a sentence requires quotation marks, and everybody putting words together in the United States should know that commas and periods always slip themselves inside the closing quotation marks ("like this," and "like so.") and that semicolons and colons park themselves outside ("get out"; and "stay out":).

Once in a great while, though, a sentence can't do without three punctuation marks in a row. Such a sentence typically (1) includes a title (such as that of a book, a movie, or a play) ending with a question mark or an exclamation point, (2) appears in a periodical that routinely encloses titles between quotation marks, and (3) either presents the title as a throwaway appositive or offers a throwaway appositive after the title (see Chapters 66-69). In a sentence of that sort, a writer committed to setting off the appositive with commas must punctuate the title by inserting a comma between the question mark or exclamation point and the closing quotation mark. It's easy, though, for the writer to fumble the punctuation—either by omitting that crucial comma or by mispositioning it.

 Its title, "How About Never—Is Never Good for You?," comes from a famous Mankoff cartoon.... (*New York Times*)

 Its title, "How About Never—Is Never Good for You?," comes from a famous Mankoff cartoon....

 ...the stars, singers and dancers of "Hello, Dolly!," the first Broadway musical to play in a war zone, were still enthralled by the experience. ([Sumter, South Carolina] *Daily Item*)

 ..."Hello, Dolly!," the first Broadway musical to play in a war zone....

Punctuational threesomes make some writers so uncomfortable that when the title is followed by an explanatory but nonessential phrase or clause calling for a comma to set it off, they feel reluctant to supply the comma.

 That's precisely what happens to Peter Chelsom's "Shall We Dance?," a remake of a balsa-light Japanese movie.... ([New York] *Daily News*)

 That's precisely what happens to Peter Chelsom's "Shall We Dance?," a remake....

Similarly, when the title is positioned at the end of an introductory phrase or adverbial dependent clause, writers sometimes can't bring themselves to furnish a comma to mark the boundary between the introductory element and the independent clause.

 Entitled "Tiny Mummies! The True Story of the Ruler of 43rd Street's Land of the Walking Dead!," the feature was every bit the unrestrained romp of tabloid journalism that Shawn had feared. (*J. D. Salinger: A Life* [Random House], by Kenneth Slawenski)

Entitled "Tiny Mummies! The True Story of the Ruler of 43rd Street's Land of the Walking Dead!," the feature was every bit the unrestrained romp....

Sentences including titles that end in question marks and exclamation points aren't the only sentences in which three-ply punctuation is inevitable. The positioning within a sentence of a direct quotation that ends with such a punctuation mark often dictates that there be three correctly situated marks in a row. If such a quotation is throwaway phrasing or appears at the end of throwaway phrasing (see Chapters 66-67 and 70-73), a comma must follow the question mark or exclamation point.

 Zappa used one of Varèse's characteristically febrile quotes, "The present-day composer refuses to die!" as an epigraph.... (*The Rock Snob's Dictionary* [Broadway Books], by David Kamp and Steven Daly)

 Zappa used one of Varèse's characteristically febrile quotes, "The present-day composer refuses to die!," as an epigraph....

 The makers of the apps, whose quizzes ask questions like "Is your friend's butt cute?" couldn't be reached for comment. (*Wall Street Journal*)

 The makers of the apps, whose quizzes ask questions like "Is your friend's butt cute?," couldn't be reached for comment.

A Miscellany of Malpractice

91 Capital Offenses

Most—and sometimes even all—of the words in the title of a book, a song, a film, or some other work merit the star treatment of capitalization. The rules governing which words deserve such preferential care, however, are not always honored.

Distressingly widespread, for instance, is the lowercasing of short verbs, such as *is*, *am*, and *was*. In the following examples, *is* and *was* demand to be capitalized.

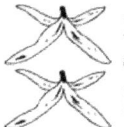

> Michelle Orange's recent debut essay collection, *This is Running for Your Life*, is another set of acrobatic associations fueled by longing. (*New Republic*)

> [title of article] Proust Wasn't a Neuroscientist. Neither was Jonah Lehrer. (*New York*)

Maybe the source of the proliferative lowercasing of *is*, *am*, and *was* is the mistaken notion that all short words call for lowercasing. True, as we'll see, most peewee words rarely deserve capitalization. But distinctions must be preserved.

All verbs, regardless of length, always claim capitalized status. The same holds true for verbals—words derived from verbs but functioning as different parts of speech. Verbals come in three varieties: the gerund, a verbal noun (always ending in *ing*), such as *Haunting* in *The Haunting of Hill House*; the participle, a verbal adjective, of which there are three types (the present participle, such as *Sheltering* in *The Sheltering Sky*; the regular past participle, always ending in *ed*, such as *Collected* in *The Collected Stories of Amy Hempel*; and the irregular past participle, such as *Gone* in "Nashville Gone to Ashes"); and the infinitive, which always consists of two words: the stem, or main form of the verb, preceded by *to* (not a preposition here but, in grammatical jargon, the sign of the infinitive, which is never capitalized [as in *Here to Get My Baby Out of Jail*] unless it's the first word of a title [as in *To Kill a Mockingbird*]).

The first word and the final word of a title are always capitalized, even if they would be lowercased anywhere else in a title. Nouns, pronouns, adjectives, and adverbs are always capitalized, no matter where they appear in a title. The articles *a*, *an*, and *the* are capitalized only if they're positioned as the first word in a title or subtitle.

Capitalization gets trickier with conjunctions and prepositions. A coordinating conjunction (such as *and* or *but*) is never capitalized unless it's the first word of a title or subtitle. Subordinating conjunctions (such as *if*, *while*, and *because*) are typically capitalized regardless of length. Conjunctive adverbs (such as *however*, *thus*, and *also*) rarely appear in titles but must be capitalized when they do.

Publishers differ on the matter of how long a preposition must be before it requires capitalization, but most agree on either a four-letter or a five-letter minimum. Standard practice for headlines in *The New York Times* is to capitalize prepositions of four or more letters. At the *The New Yorker*, the general policy is to capitalize any preposition at least five letters long.

Some words that ordinarily function as prepositions can function adverbially in a phrasal verb or a phrasal verbal, which consists of a verb (or verbal) followed by a preposition playing the role of an adverb. Prepositions in adverbial drag require capitalization, as in *Woke Up Lonely*. If the preposition playing the part of an adverb is attached to a participle to form an adjectival compound modifying a noun, capitalize the adverb and attach it to the participle with a hyphen, as in *Picked-Up Pieces*.

Finally, the words *who, whom, whose, that, which, how*, and *what* are always capitalized.

92 A friend of mine is confused about capitalization: She [*she?*] wants to know whether to capitalize the first word of the equivalent of a complete declarative sentence (which may include an introductory phrase or introductory dependent clause) that follows a colon if the colon is preceded by the equivalent of a complete sentence.

The answer to your friend's question?

It depends.

With a couple of universally all-purpose exceptions discussed later, *The New Yorker*, for example, doesn't capitalize the first word in such constructions—except when the first word is a proper noun or a proper adjective (such as *Renata Adler* or *Adlerian*), which always requires capitalization, or the pronoun *I*. At the opposite extreme, *New York* magazine does capitalize the first word. *The New York Times* now routinely capitalizes the first word, and so does *The Wall Street Journal*, though inconsistencies appear in both. Unless you're writing for a publication whose style manual requires upper- or lowercasing, you're free to choose whichever style you prefer. What's important is consistency.

That said, however, there are some sentences in which capitalization is always required after a colon, some in which capitalization is always out of the question, and some in which it's left to the writer's discretion unless she's writing for a publication that prescribes how the capitalization of phrasing following a colon should be handled.

First, if the independent clause preceding the colon is preparing the reader for two or more consecutive sentences that are elaborating on or providing examples of the statement in the independent clause, you need to capitalize the first word of each of the sentences that are covered overhead, so to speak, by the umbrella of that first independent clause.

Square Wallet, an innovative new app, is changing the way we spend our money. Here's how it works: you link your credit or debit card to the app, shop, take your items to a cashier at a participating retailer and, as the company's Web site says, "simply say your name at checkout to pay." Your name and photograph appear on the register, the cashier gives you a nod, and you walk happily out the door with your artisan shade-grown organic coffee. (*New York Times*)

Quick fix: capitalize the first word after the colon.

Second, when a colon is followed by a series of related questions, each question must begin with an uppercased letter.

 Three questions popped into her head: Why me? Why now? What next?

Third, the first word of any phrasing that does not amount to the equivalent of a complete sentence must never be capitalized (unless it's a proper noun, a proper adjective, or the pronoun *I*) when it follows a colon that is preceded by an independent clause.

 [the colon is followed by a series of gerundial phrases] This is more or less how every workday begins for Kimmel: Blurring the line between domestic life and job life, turning the breakfast table into an extension of the show, making work feel less like a grind and more like hanging out with people he loves. (*Rolling Stone*)

Quick fix: lowercase the *b* in *Blurring*.

 [the colon is followed by a long infinitive phrase] So the Bugamis are planning the once unthinkable: To have their toddler undergo bariatric surgery to permanently remove part of his stomach in hopes of reducing his appetite and staving off a lifetime of health problems. (*Wall Street Journal*)

Quick fix: lowercase the *t* in *To* following the colon.

Fourth, when the colon is preceded by phrasing that lacks the grammatical status of an independent clause (phrasing such as *a word of warning, a word to the wise, first things first, among the findings,* and *note to self*) but is followed by an independent clause (the equivalent of a grammatically complete sentence), publishing-world practice varies as to whether the first word of the phrasing following the colon should be capitalized (unless, of course, the first word is one that always requires capitalization).

The New Yorker lowercases after such phrasing, and *New York* magazine capitalizes, but *The New York Times* and *The Wall Street Journal* are often inconsistent. (Phrasing following the introductory element and not functioning as the equivalent of an independent clause, however, never begins with a capital letter unless the first word is one that always requires capitalization, as in *One advantage: Costco's higher wages.*) So how should *you* manage the capitalization? Again, unless you're writing for a publication whose style manual lays down the law, it's a matter of your preference—and a matter of being consistent. This book, however, recommends *New Yorker* style: lowercasing. If the phrase preceding the colon, however, is followed by two or more sentences elaborating on or explaining what was introduced in the phrase, you'll need to capitalize the first word of each of the elaborative or explanatory sentences that follow the colon.

Finally, when the colon following an independent clause is directing the reader toward a quotation, the first word of the quotation is capitalized.

 The reviewer cited a statement by Roland Barthes: "The writer is someone who arranges quotes and removes the quotation marks."

93 The Trouble Between *Among* and *Between*

The dust-jacket biographies of authors often state that a writer divides her time between, say, Brooklyn and Ann Arbor. But what if she buys a summer house in Barnegat Bay, New Jersey? Does she now divide her time *among* Brooklyn, Ann Arbor, and Barnegat Bay, New Jersey?

No.

If most people remember anything about how the preposition *between* differs from *among*, it's that the former is used when discussing two things or people and the latter is used when discussing three or more. One speaks of a secret shared between Jorie and her sister and of a joke shared among several friends. But the distinction between the two prepositions doesn't end there. *Among* is used appropriately when three or more persons or things are not all interacting individually with the others, as in *The manager did everything she could to foster team spirit among her employees.* If all of the three or more persons or things (such as A, B, and C), however, are in fact interacting one-on-one with the others (A with B, A with C, B with C), only *between* makes any sense.

There was a growing unease among the three sisters means that all three share something, but there's no emphasis on the sisters as individuals. *There was increasing hostility between the three sisters*, however, means that each sister felt increasingly hostile toward each of the other two; the emphasis is on the individuals. *Between* pinpoints persons or things one at a time; *among* waves rather abstractly or indefinitely at whatever three or more persons or things have in common without singling out any one in particular. *Among* is inclusive in its embrace; *between* is exclusive, putting its finger on one member of the group before moving on to the next.

 Rather than take the shuttle among the buildings, he drives his car to save minutes. (*New Yorker*)

No matter how many buildings there are at the site, the shuttle travels not among them but between them (that is, between Building A and Building B, then between Building B and Building C, and so on).

Quick fix: substitute *between* for *among*.

94 Let sleeping dogs lie—*not* lay.

The misuse of *lay* for *lie*, of *laying* for *lying*, and of *laid* for *lay* is no longer confined to the semiliterate.

 ...she would lay awake in frustration.... (*New York*)

 What now lays in storage is an assemblage of garments.... (*Wall Street Journal*)

Authorities reportedly found the makeup artist's body laying on the sidewalk.... (huffingtonpost.com)

 *...he laid awake at night worrying about Fiat employees....* (*New York Times*)

In those excerpts, *lie* should be substituted for *lay*, *lies* for *lays*, *lying* for *laying*, and *lay* for *laid*.

So how might we unmuddle the distinction between *lie* and *lay*? As you ease yourself onto a futon after a long day, you are about to lie, not lay. Keep that long *i* of *lie* foremost in your mind: *I'm inclined to recline supine.* Tonight you will lie, but yesterday you lay. It's that simple: *lay* is the past-tense form of *lie*.

Easy enough, no?

The trouble is that *lay* is not only the past-tense form of the verb *lie*. The combination of letters forming *lay* also constitutes another verb in our language, a verb entirely different from *lie*.

To lay means to place something somewhere—to situate it other than where it was. *Lay* is the present-tense form, and *laid* is the past-tense form: *I want to lay my head on her shoulder. She laid her briefcase on the bed.*

It might be time to slip in a little grammatical terminology.

The present-tense *lay* and the past-tense *laid* are transitive verbs: verbs that always take a direct object. That is, they're always followed by a noun or a pronoun: *She will lay her head on the pillow.* (The direct object is *head*.) *She laid the can of Mace on the counter.* (The direct object is *can*.)

The verb *to lie*, in contrast, is intransitive. That means *lie* (or its past-tense form, *lay*) never takes a direct object. It will never be followed by a noun or a pronoun. But it might be followed by a single-word adverb (such as *quietly* or *down*): *She is going to lie down.* Or it might be followed by an adverbial prepositional phrase (such as *on her side*): *She lay on her side.*

To sum up, let's say you're in the present tense. To use the verb *lay* correctly, you're going to have to *do* something *to* something: you're going to have to put something down somewhere. In short, you'll be active, at least to a degree. But if you're going to use the word *lie* correctly, you're finally done with doing things to things—at least for now. You've had it with action. So go lie down.

If you're someone who lives in the past, though, you'll be using *laid* correctly only if you did something to something: you already laid your clothes out for tomorrow. You'll be using *lay* correctly only if you were earlier stretched out.

Finally, the past participle of *lie* is *lain*, but it's rarely used in this casual age. So instead of saying *She had lain in bed for days*, you could say *She had been lying in bed for days*. The past participle of *lay*, though, is the same as its past-tense form. In *She laid it on the line*, *laid* is the simple-past tense form, but in *She had laid things out as plainly as possible*, *laid* is a past participle.

95

I graduated college like I was supposed to, so why can't I reduce the amount of errors that effect how others see me? I could of studied more, and I read less books than everybody else, but it's not that big of a deal. As far as my reading, is that a fair criteria to judge me by? You can't convince me to change.

First, you graduate *from* a school. The following sentence desperately needs the preposition.

 He did introduce her to Ryan, who had moved to New Jersey after graduating college. (*New Yorker*)

Second, in all but the most casual prose, avoid using *like* as a subordinating conjunction; replace *like* with *as if* (occasionally, *as, that,* or *the way* will do instead). The writer of the following sentence gets things right only in the final dependent clause.

 The height of style is no style, to dress like you did not bother to get dressed at all, like your closet consists of exactly one perfectly fitting T-shirt, one broken-in but quietly tailored pair of jeans, one chambray or denim shirt that looks as if you lifted it from your grandfather's closet, and not much more. (*New York Times*)

Third, maintain the traditional distinction between *amount* and *number*.

 …the amount of employees who consider work-life balance very important to their overall job satisfaction continues to increase. (forbes.com)

What the writer means is the *number* of employees. Use *number* when a quantity is divisible into individual, countable units: *the number of women*. Use *amount* when a quantity or mass is not divisible into countable units: *the amount of work*.

A similar distinction obtains between *less* and *fewer*. Use *fewer* much as you would use *number*—when there are countable units involved. Use *less* when a quantity cannot be divided into countable units: *less tofu*.

 His work inspired no less than 70 films. (*Wall Street Journal*)

Quick fix: substitute *fewer* for *less*.

Fourth, something isn't that big of a deal—it's simply not that big a deal. The preposition *of* has no place in such phrasing.

 It doesn't sound like the most glamorous task in the larger effort of conquering the final frontier, or maybe even that big of a problem. (*New York Times*)

Sadder still is the screamingly ungrammatical substitution of the preposition *of* for the helping verb *have* (or its contracted form: *'ve*) in *could of, should of, would of, may of, might of,* and *must of*.

 Fortunately, both the teams that should of won, did prevail. (huffingtonpost.com)

Fifth, the phrasing *as far as* functions as a subordinating conjunction, not as a preposition. It's used correctly only when it's followed by both a subject and a predicate (such as *is* [or *are*] *concerned* or *goes* [or *go*]). It's used incorrectly if it's followed by only a noun or a pronoun.

 Kozar said "everything is on the table" as far as budget cuts, but a line has to be drawn somewhere. ([Greensburg, PA] *Tribune-Review*)

Quick fix: ... as far as budget cuts are concerned....

In a sentence such as *As far as the budget cuts, there's no alternative,* the ungrammatical *As far as the budget cuts* can be converted to a prepositional phrase: *As for the budget cuts, there's no alternative.*

Sixth, a standard by which we judge someone or something is a criterion. The noun *criterion* is singular. The plural form is *criteria.*

 No, the sole criteria that has gotten these individuals nominated is their wealth.... (*Wall Street Journal*)

Quick fix: substitute *criterion* for *criteria.*

Similarly, *phenomena* is increasingly used as if it were a singular noun.

 In this respect it resembles averted vision, a phenomena familiar to backyard astronomers.... (*New York Times*)

Quick fix: substitute *phenomenon* for *phenomena.*

Seventh, you can't convince anybody 'to do anything, but you can at least try to persuade her. *Convince,* when used correctly, is never followed by an infinitive; it's most commonly followed either by an indirect object and a nominative dependent clause (*She convinced Josh that he needs a smaller apartment*) or by a direct object and one or more prepositional phrases (*She convinced Lisa of the importance of volunteering*). *Persuade,* which means *urge,* is correctly followed by a subject of an infinitive and then the infinitive itself (*She persuaded Lisa to vote*).

Substitute *persuade* for *convince* in the following sentence.

 Now she has a single weekend in which she must convince, or beg, them to change their minds.... (*New Yorker*)

Finally, as for *affect* versus *effect,* let's skip the specialized uses of these words that come into play only infrequently (consult a dictionary if you're interested—and let's hope you are) and instead review what the words mean in everyday usage.

 ... they were aware that the concerns expressed by others were having an affect on him. (*New York Times*)

The writer needs *effect.*

 "... it's going to effect the children ...," she said. (*New York Times*)

The writer needs *affect.*

To *affect* means *to cause a change in* or *to have an influence on. Affect* is a verb. *Effect* is a noun meaning *result* or *consequence.*